Penguin Education

Penguin Modern Economic Texts
General Editor: B. J. McCormick

International Economics
Editor: J. Spraos

Trade and Specialization

Ronald Findlay

Penguin Modern Economics Texts

General Editor:
B. J. McCormick
Senior Lecturer in Economics
University of Sheffield

Development Economics
Editor: P. Robson
Professor of Economics
St Salvator's College
University of St Andrews

Econometrics
Editor: G. R. Fisher
Professor of Econometrics
University of Southampton

Economic Thought
Editor: K. J. W. Alexander
Professor of Economics
University of Strathclyde

Industrial Economics
Editor: H. Townsend
Reader in Economics
London School of Economics
and Political Science
University of London

International Economics
Editor: J. Spraos
Professor of Economics
University College London

Labour Economics
Editor: K. J. W. Alexander
Professor of Economics
University of Strathclyde

Macroeconomics
Editor: R. W. Clower
Professor of Economics
Northwestern University
Illinois

Microeconomics
Editor: B. J. McCormick
Senior Lecturer in Economics
University of Sheffield

Political Economy
Editor: K. J. W. Alexander
Professor of Economics
University of Strathclyde

Trade and Specialization

Ronald Findlay

Penguin Books

Penguin Books Ltd, Harmondsworth,
Middlesex, England
Penguin Books Inc., 7110 Ambassador Road,
Baltimore, Md 21207, U.S.A.
Penguin Books Australia Ltd,
Ringwood, Victoria, Australia

First published 1970
Reprinted 1971

Made and printed in Great Britain by
Cox & Wyman Ltd, London, Reading and Fakenham
Set in Monotype Times

To H.G.J.

Penguin Modern Economics Texts

This volume is one in a series of unit texts designed to reduce the price of knowledge for students of economics in universities and colleges of higher education. The units may be used singly or in combination with other units to form attractive and unusual teaching programmes. The volumes will cover the major teaching areas but they will differ from conventional books in their attempt to chart and explore new directions in economic thinking. The traditional divisions of theory and applied, of positive and normative and of micro and macro will tend to be blurred as authors impose new and arresting ideas on the traditional corpus of economics. Some units will fall into conventional patterns of thought but many will transgress established beliefs.

Penguin Modern Economics Texts are published in units in order to achieve certain objectives. First, a large range of short texts at inexpensive prices gives the teacher flexibility in planning his course and recommending texts for it. Secondly, the pace at which important new work is published requires the project to be adaptable. Our plan allows a unit to be revised or a fresh unit to be added with maximum speed and minimal cost to the reader.

The international range of authorship will, it is hoped, bring out the richness and diversity in economic analysis and thinking.

B.J.MCC.

Contents

Editorial Foreword

This textbook is one of many which will attempt to cover between them the main concepts and topics in International Economics. *Balance-of-payments Policy* and *The International Monetary System* have already appeared; others will follow.

International Economics is the oldest branch of Economics viewed as a discipline and the second oldest (after Public Finance) viewed as an area of practical concern for a national economy. The first extant account of England's balance of trade goes back to 1355! It hardly needs saying, however, that it is not for antiquarian reasons that International Economics commands attention at the present time. Any alert citizen knows that some of the most intractable economic problems are international in character.

This volume covers an area which lies at the core of trade theory. It is concerned with the pattern of trade – the hypotheses which attempt to explain this pattern and the empirical evidence available on this subject. The best economists have been attracted to this area by the fundamental character of the questions involved, and the literature on the subject is vast and sophisticated. Professor Findlay captures in this small volume both the vastness and the sophistication with rare expository skill.

J. S.

Preface

This book is one of a series on International Economics. It is intended for undergraduate students who have a good foundation in economic theory and for beginning graduate students. It is hoped that the level of presentation is appropriate for this objective. Mathematical formulae have been kept to a minimum but there is a liberal use of diagrams. The reader not already familiar with the material covered will probably need pencil and paper to draw his own diagrams as he goes along as much of the text can be described as 'verbal geometry'. Although the scope of the book has been confined to the foundations of the subject matter, the pure theory of international specialization and trade has been developing so fast that many of the results discussed are fresh from the periodical literature of the last few years. For help in the writing of this book I am grateful to Professor John Spraos for his valuable editorial comments on the choice of topics and level of presentation, to U Myat Thein, my former colleague at the Institute of Economics, Rangoon, for several stimulating discussions and useful suggestions, particularly in connexion with chapter 4, and to my wife for constantly reminding a lazy writer of his obligation to complete the manuscript. They are not of course to be held responsible for the many shortcomings that remain in spite of their kind efforts.

1 Introduction

Problems of international trade and finance have always been among the most momentous and controversial of issues in economic debate. One readily thinks of mercantilism, the Corn Laws, imperial preference and German reparations in the past and in contemporary economic discussion there are all the vexed questions connected with the European common market, the Kennedy round, UNCTAD, international liquidity and so on. The theory of international trade is a complex structure of thought that has developed over the last two centuries or so largely in response to the problems posed by these controversial issues. As with any scheme of thought there has been an internal logic in the evolution of ideas but this development has always been stimulated and influenced by the major policy questions of the day. The most creative periods in the scientific development of the subject have been closely connected with crucial turning points in the world system of trade and payments. Thus Hume's theory of the specie-flow mechanism and the Ricardian theory of comparative advantage were developed at a time when free trade was beginning to replace mercantilism as the accepted framework for national trading policies. The theory of exchange rates and the Keynesian theory of balance-of-payments ajustment both arose in response to the disintegration of the international financial system based on the gold standard in the inter-war years. At present the problems of regional trade groupings, the reconciliation of internal with external stabilization policies and the trading difficulties of the developing countries are all exercising the minds of economists and the theory of international trade is advancing rapidly as a result.

The reader who has cursorily followed even the journalism on these contemporary controversies is bound to discover that 'the advantages of international specialization' or some similar phrase is always being invoked by at least one side in the argument if not both. Thus customs unions such as the European common market may be blessed for getting the world closer to universal free trade and the pattern of specialization resulting therefrom in so far as tariffs between members are removed, or they may be cursed for getting further away from that ideal in so far as tariffs against non-members are raised. Advocates for the cause of the developing countries argue that the 'colonial pattern' of specialization worked against the interest of these countries in the past and hence that they should be allowed to impose tariffs and other restrictions on imports from the advanced countries while enjoying free access to the markets of these countries in the future. Those economists who are anxious about the scarcity of international liquidity argue that the benefits of international specialization will be lost if countries restrict to protect their reserves, while their opponents argue that these same benefits will be eroded by 'exported inflation' unless the 'discipline of gold' is maintained. It should therefore be clear that without a grasp of the theory of international specialization one cannot make much sense of the controversies on these vital issues of the day.

The first scientific demonstration of how international trade can be beneficial to all partners was by David Ricardo in 1817, using a simple numerical example involving trade between England and Portugal in cloth and wine. He showed that so long as the relative unit costs of the two commodities differed between the two countries trade between them would take place, each country exporting the commodity that it could produce relatively more cheaply, and that this trade would be mutually beneficial. With this demonstration, and also using arguments of a dynamic nature involving the favourable effect of lower real wages on profits and capital accumulation, Ricardo and his followers provided the intellectual foundation of the successful attack on the Corn Laws. Theory and policy were thus intertwined from the outset, and the association between the classical theory of international trade and free trade policies has continued to be close in spite of a series of logical breaches in the classical case for free trade.

Developments in the century and a half since Ricardo have replaced the magnificent simplicity of his original demonstration with a vastly more elaborate logical structure and also in recent years with a rapidly growing volume of empirical data for the testing of the hypotheses of the theory. It can, however, be said that there has been a basic continuity of development, with the later contributions filling gaps in the original argument rather than drastically altering the assumptions or controverting the logic of the classical pioneers.

Several of the major assumptions of the classical theory such as perfectly competitive markets, the absence of transport costs, the complete mobility of factors within countries and immobility between countries are still made in the basic formulations of the modern theory, although there are a number of *ad hoc* studies dealing with the effects of market imperfections, immigration and so on. The crudeness of the labour theory of value as an analytical tool limited Ricardo to consideration of the constant cost case whereas the modern theory is able to handle quite easily the more general case of increasing cost. The decreasing cost case, which is of considerable interest for underdeveloped countries beginning their industrialization, still, however, presents major problems of analysis and only very limited progress has been made in dealing with it. This generalization of the cost assumptions by the modern theory has brought with it a shift of emphasis from the cost ratios themselves to the more basic determinants of these ratios, which are the national endowments of productive factors, technology and the pattern of demand. Within this broader framework the Ricardian hypothesis can be interpreted as specifying that international differences in technology of a 'neutral' type are the crucial factor in determining the structure of trade. Since the inter-war years, however, the alternative view of the Swedish economists Eli Heckscher and Bertil Ohlin, that it is differences in factor endowment that are the main cause of trade, has attracted much more attention. Until very recently another major classical assumption, that national factor endowments are fixed, has continued to be made in most discussions of trade theory. A growing body of work on the effects of changes in factor endowment and technology on trade has now, however, appeared.

In 1929 Professor J. H. Williams (1929) delivered a scathing attack on the assumptions of the theory of international trade, particularly those of fixed resources and absence of international factor mobility. Although, as has been said, some progress has been made in relaxing these assumptions the modern methodological position is not to defend the 'realism' of the assumptions of the theory but rather to test its implications. It is in this direction that remarkable progress has been made in recent years.

The main difference in approach between the classical and modern views on the theory of international trade lies in the explicit separation, in the latter case, of the 'positive' parts of the doctrine which relate to empirically refutable hypotheses on the structure of trade from the 'normative' parts concerned with the benefits or gains from trade, which depend upon the meta-economic criteria that are used for their evaluation. This separation has developed in line with the increasing rigour and sophistication of modern welfare economics, which since the time of Pareto early in this century has been meticulously removing the value judgements that earlier writers illegitimately imported into their assessment of the properties of models of competitive equilibrium, of which the classical theory of international trade is an example. Accordingly questions such as the sense in which trade is superior to autarky, or the relationship between the gains to be obtained from free trade in comparison with some degree of restricted trade are now approached with much more awareness of their dependence on ethical judgements about the distribution of income between individuals than was the case before. Policy recommendations are also made much less sweepingly than before, reflecting this greater methodological sophistication.

The objective of this book is to present, in a concise but fairly rigorous form, the foundations of that part of the theory of international trade which deals with the explanation of the pattern of international specialization and the gains from trade. The treatment will be along analytical rather than historical lines, the brief discussion in this first chapter having to suffice for perspective on the development of the doctrine. The reader interested in *Dogmengeschichte* can turn to the classic study of Professor Viner (1937) and also to the later volume by Richard Caves (1960). Contemporary developments are very well reviewed in a survey article by J. Bhagwati (1964). Monetary problems connected with exchange rates and the balance of payments, the theory of tariffs and customs unions, and the problems of trade and the developing countries will be covered by other volumes in this series.

Five chapters follow. The next chapter will first give a self-contained presentation of the two-factor, two-commodity general equilibrium model of resource allocation and production that has long served as the basic analytical tool in the theory of international trade. The determination of international equilibrium in a two-country model of trade is then depicted in a manner analogous to the traditional 'supply and demand' approach to the problem of equilibrium in a closed economy. Finally it is shown how world equilibrium will be achieved in a many-country model.

Trade will always arise between countries if there is any difference in the relative costs of commodities at the margin. This proposition is proved in chapter 2 but the question of what factors can be considered as the determinants of these comparative cost differences is dealt with systematically in chapter 3. Factor endowments, technology and tastes vary between countries and any or all of these differences is a sufficient cause for trade to flow between nations. Special attention is devoted to the Ricardian theory, which makes technological differences the basic cause of trade and the Heckscher-Ohlin theory which sees differences in relative factor endowment as playing the major role.

In considering the impact of trade on the development of colonial economies in South-East Asia and Africa Hla Myint has felt that the 'vent for surplus' view of international trade put forward by Adam Smith is a superior framework of analysis to Ricardian and post-Ricardian comparative advantage models. Irving Kravis has asserted that the geographic availability or non-availability of essential requirements for the production of goods, such as natural resources of particular types, is the main influence on trade and not the relative costs of capital and labour. Several writers have also put forward the view that in the exports of industrial countries, which constitute the bulk of world exports, technological innovation in the form of the introduction of new goods is the dominant factor, trade taking place until other countries learn the technology and start producing the goods themselves. These 'vent for surplus', 'availability' and 'imitation gap' theories are examined in chapter 4.

The formulation of theoretical hypotheses is essential for the scientific study of any subject but this activity needs to be combined with empirical testing of the hypotheses if it is to be more than barren speculation. Recently great progress has been made in this respect, starting with pioneering contributions by Sir Donald MacDougall and Professor Wassily Leontief on the Ricardian and Heckscher-Ohlin theories respectively. The results so far achieved are examined and their implications for the validity or otherwise of the alternative theories of the basis for trade are assessed in chapter 5.

The final chapter deals with the welfare implications of trade – the question of the 'gains from trade' or the sense in which trade results in making the world as a whole or a particular country 'better off'. The classical approach is examined briefly and after its inadequacies have been pointed out the modern formulation stemming from the 1939 analysis by Samuelson is developed. The basic concepts of modern welfare economics required are explained in the process.

This book does not attempt anything like a complete coverage of the entire theory of international specialization and the gains from trade. That would require a volume many times larger. What is intended is to present the basic framework of the theory and the major empirical research relevant to the testing of the theory in a logically rigorous but mathematically elementary way. The main analytical tools are therefore diagrams but recourse is had to algebra and differential calculus in one or two instances. The reader who desires an introduction to the growing body of mathematically advanced treatments of the subject is referred to a massive and erudite three-part survey article by J. S. Chipman (1965, 1966).

Considerations of space have also forced the exclusion of any treatment of transport costs and location, monopolistic influences and several other topics. This is not done in the belief that these matters are unimportant but simply reflects the fact that these problems have not as yet been successfully integrated into the main body of doctrine, to which this book is an introduction.

2 The General Equilibrium of Resource Allocation, Production and Trade

A theory of international trade must always take as its starting point a theory of resource allocation and production for a closed economy. In the case of Ricardo this was the classical labour theory of value. In the case of the modern doctrine it is the theory of general equilibrium, which embraces the labour theory of value as a special case. We shall therefore begin this chapter with the analysis of resource allocation and production in a closed economy, using two geometric tools that are very widely employed by trade theorists: the production transformation curve introduced by Haberler in 1930, and the production 'box diagram' introduced by Stolper and Samuelson in 1941 but adapted from the analogous consumption box diagram of Edgeworth and Bowley. Next we shall introduce international trade between one country and the 'rest of the world,' and show how the equilibrium terms of trade and export-import volumes are determined. The analysis is then extended to any number of countries.

The Transformation Curve and the Box Diagram

If the productive resources and technical knowledge available to an economy are taken as fixed, these limitations will result in less of some good being produced if more of another is. We can therefore conceive of alternative sets of production levels for the different goods corresponding to the different uses to which the fixed resources and technology are put. If the different goods are limited to two (which may be thought of as broad aggregates such as agricultural goods and manufactures) the situation can be depicted graphically as in Figure 1.

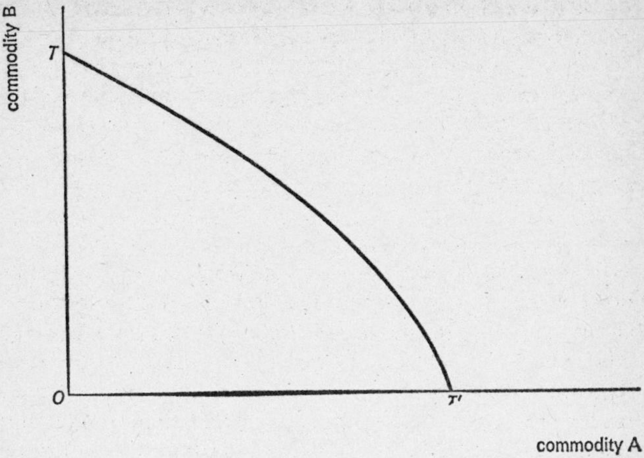

Figure 1

The curve TT' shows the various combinations of the commodities A and B that can be produced with the given resources and technology. As more of one good is produced less resources are available for the other so that its production must be reduced. Points inside TT' are inefficient in the sense that more of at least one good can be obtained without less of the other, while points outside are unattainable. The concave shape of the curve reflects the assumption that as we add successive equal increments of one good we have to give up increasingly larger quantities of the other. One possible reason for this type of 'diminishing returns' is that, as the substitution takes place, resources that are less and less suitable for the production of the expanding commodity, and more and more suitable for the production of the contracting commodity, are being shifted over with the result that the 'opportunity cost' of the resources needed to produce one unit of the expanding commodity, measured by the decline that is caused in the production of the contracting commodity, gets increasingly larger. As the substitution of production takes place along the curve we can conceive of the production of one commodity being 'transformed' into that of the other which explains the name of transformation curve given to this construction. The slope of the curve at any point, which measures the opportunity cost of producing one more unit of one commodity in terms of the other, is referred to as the marginal rate of transformation.

The dependence of the transformation curve on the amounts of the fixed resources and the technology available is brought out explicitly by the production box diagram. Assuming that there are only two factors of production (let us call them land and labour) we can represent the technology or 'production function' of each good by an 'isoquant map' or family of constant product curves showing the various combinations of land and labour with which it is possible to produce any given level of output. The isoquants for both goods are assumed to be smooth and convex to the origin, implying the possibility of continuous substitution of one factor for another but at a diminishing rate. The reader may consult any elementary textbook for a fuller discussion of the nature and properties of these curves. If the total amounts of land and labour available are given we can construct the box diagram as shown in Figure 2.

Let $OX (= O'Y)$ represent the amount of land available and $OY (= O'X)$ the amount of labour. The isoquant map for A is drawn from the origin O while the isoquant map for B is inverted and drawn from the origin O'. Corresponding to any point in the box will be four co-ordinates showing the land and labour used for the production of each commodity, the total land and labour used for both commodities always being equal to the fixed amounts available. The production level for each commodity corresponding to a point in the box can be read off from the respective isoquants which pass through it. Every point in the box therefore determines a *feasible* pair of production levels for the two goods, in the sense that sufficient amounts of the two factors are available to make them attainable for the economy.

Out of this entire set of feasible points there is a subset of particular significance – the points which are efficient in the sense that for a given output of one commodity the output of the other is maximized. Consider the point *m*; if we move to the left along the same A isoquant that passes through it we will be crossing successively higher B isoquants until we reach the point *n* at which the B isoquant has a common tangent to the A isoquant that passes through *m*. Thus as we move from *m* to *n* the output of B keeps rising while the output of A remains constant. The point *n* therefore is an efficient point since for the given level of A production it has the maximum possible

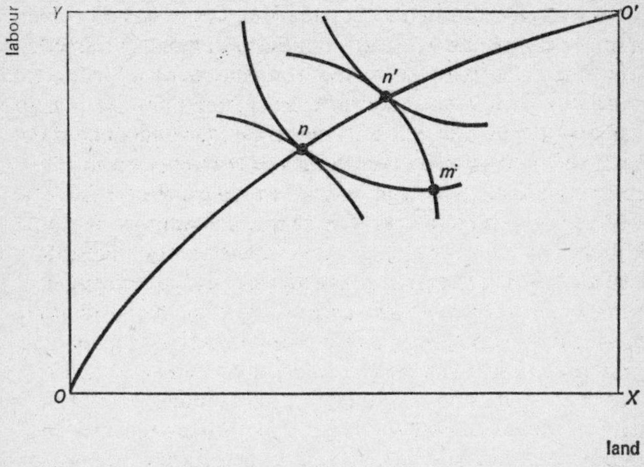

Figure 2

production of B. It can now be readily seen that the set of all efficient points corresponds to the locus OO', at each point of which there is a common tangent to an A and a B isoquant. This locus is called the 'efficiency-locus'. The output levels of A and B corresponding to each point on the efficiency-locus can be shown on a separate diagram with these variables as the axes and the result is nothing but a transformation curve like TT' in Figure 1. We have therefore shown how the transformation curve can be *derived* directly from the box diagram.

The slope of a tangent to an isoquant measures the ratios of the marginal productivities of the two factors or what is known as the *marginal rate of substitution* between the factors, i.e. the amount of one factor that must be substituted for one unit of the other if output is to remain constant. Since each point on the efficiency-locus has a common tangent to an A and a B isoquant, it follows that the marginal rates of substitution between labour and land are equal for the two goods all along this curve, whereas they are unequal for any point off the locus. The necessity for the marginal rates of substitution to be equal if resources are to be allocated efficiently can be easily appreciated by the following numerical example. Suppose that the marginal rate of substitution is three labour for one land in A and two labour for one land in B. Then if one land is transferred from B to A, three units of labour can be transferred in the opposite direction, leaving the output of A unchanged. But only two of these units are required to keep B production at the former level. The remaining one unit of labour can be used to increase the output of either commodity or both of them. Since this kind of reshuffling can always take place when the marginal rates of substitution differ, equality of the rates is required for efficiency in the allocation of resources.

One problem that remains is to prove that the transformation curve derived from a box diagram will have the concave shape of the curve in Figure 1, exhibiting increasing marginal opportunity cost of production. We shall give below a simple graphical proof, resting upon the assumption that the production function for each commodity (the relationship between output and the two inputs) has the property of constant returns to scale, i.e. changing all inputs in any common proportion will change output by exactly that proportion. An important property of constant returns to scale production functions is that the marginal productivities of each factor, and hence the marginal rate of substitution, depend only upon the *ratios* in which the factors are combined. Graphically this property means that the tangents to successive isoquants at points where they are cut by a straight line through the origin (representing a given factor combination ratio) will all be parallel to each other.

Let us select any two points on the efficiency-locus in Figure 2, say n and n'. We can plot the output levels of A and B corresponding to these points as the co-ordinates of points *N* and *N′* in Figure 3. *N* and *N′* will therefore be two points on a transformation curve. For convenience let us say that the output combination represented by *N* is 60A and 100B while that represented by *N′* is 70A and 84B. Since both *N* and *N′* correspond to points on the efficiency-locus of the same box diagram it follows that the same total amounts of labour and land are used at each point.

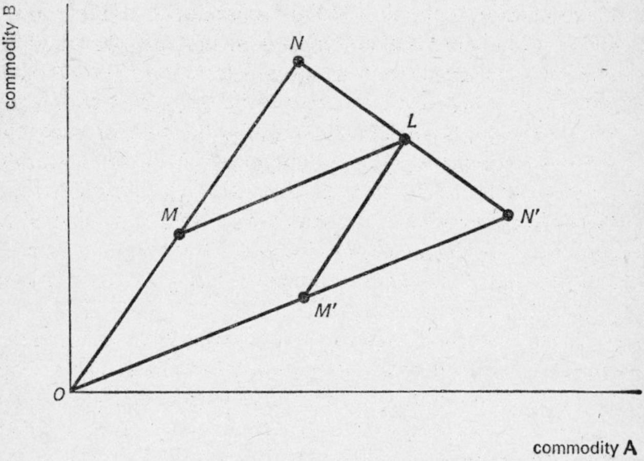

Figure 3

Suppose now that we produce only half of each output level corresponding to *N*, that is 30A and 50B, but leave the technique of production or land-labour ratio the same in each sector. Point *M* in Figure 3, half-way on the line *ON*, will correspond to production of 30A and 50B. If there are constant returns to scale halving each output with the land-labour ratios unchanged will result in the total use of land and labour at *M* being exactly half of what it is at *N*. In the same way we can find the point *M′* half-way along *ON′*, corresponding to production of 35A and 42B. The total land labour used at *M′* will also be half of what it is at *N′*. If we now *add* the production levels of A and B corresponding to the two points *M* and *M′* we will get the combination 65A and 92B. Will this combination be feasible? It is easy to see that it is, since both *M* and *M′* each use half of the labour and land used at *N* and *N′* respectively and the amounts used at *N* and *N′* are equal. The combination 65A and 92B therefore uses exactly the same amount of land and labour as those corresponding to the points *N* and *N′* and is therefore feasible.

The next step is to locate the point corresponding to 65A and 92B in Figure 3. It is readily verified that it is the point *L* lying half-way between *N* and *N′*. This is because 65A is half-way between 60A and 70A on the horizontal axis and 92B is half-way between 100B and 84B on the vertical axis.

Since the choice of *N* and *N′* is arbitrary it follows that a point half-way between *any* two points of the transformation curve must be feasible. The result does not depend on the figures chosen for illustrative purposes since the average of two numbers is always half-way between them. This implies that the transformation curve can never be convex to the origin. But can the transformation curve not be linear? We shall show that it cannot be, except under a very special condition.

Consider the feasible point *L* that we located half-way between *N* and *N′*. The 65A that is produced at this point consists of 30A produced with a labour-land ratio equal to the slope of the (undrawn) line *On* (in Figure 2) and 35A with a labour-land ratio equal to the slope of *On′*. Since the former ratio is higher, the marginal productivity of land will be higher with the first technique than with the second, and the opposite will be the case for labour; in other words, the marginal rate of factor substitution will be different for the same commodity. It follows that the transfer of land from the subsector of A using the *On′* technique to that using the *On* one will raise the output of A, and so will the transfer of labour in the opposite direction, until all the A produced is with a single technique, intermediate between *On* and *On′*, the total land and labour used for A each remaining constant. Exactly similar reasoning will show that the output of B can also be raised without an increase of either factor in that sector. Even when both A and B are each produced with a uniform technique the marginal rates of substitution will differ *between* the sectors. Hence a further re-allocation of the fixed factors will further increase the output of both goods.

Point *L* therefore cannot be efficient since it is possible to produce more of both goods than are produced at *L* with the same resources. This means that the transformation curve cannot have a linear segment and so the transformation curve itself cannot be linear. This leaves a concave transformation curve as the only remaining possibility, as was required to be proved.

There is one situation, however, in which we do get a linear transformation curve. This is if the efficiency-locus in Figure 2 corresponds to the diagonal of the box, implying that the land-labour ratio is the same for both commodities. Except for this special case we will always have a concave transformation curve if there are fixed factor supplies and constant returns to scale. Concavity will be even more pronounced in the event of diminishing returns to scale.

Equilibrium in a Closed Economy

Our analysis has so far concentrated purely on the physical or technological side. It is now time to introduce demand and prices so that the equilibrium configuration of factor allocations and output levels for the two sectors can be determined. We shall do this by means of the familiar concept of equality between demand and supply but in terms of the general equilibrium of the whole economy rather than in terms of partial equilibrium for a single industry only. For this task the assumption of perfect competition is necessary as no one has really succeeded in giving a satisfactory analysis of general equilibrium under monopolistic conditions. The essential aspect of perfect competition is that producers and consumers take prices as given and adjust their behaviour so as to maximize their profit or utility subject to this limitation.

Given the prices of land and labour firms in each sector of the economy will seek to adjust the combination of the two factors that they use so as to minimize the cost of production for any fixed level of output. Graphically the situation can be depicted as in Figures 4a and b where the lines FF' and GG' represent 'constant factor outlay lines', that is, different combinations of the two factors that have the same total cost at the given prices for each of the factors. The slope of the constant factor outlay line represents the ratio of the factor prices. The 'least cost combination' for each sector is given by the point of tangency between an isoquant and the constant factor outlay line. This means that the condition for minimizing costs is that the mar-

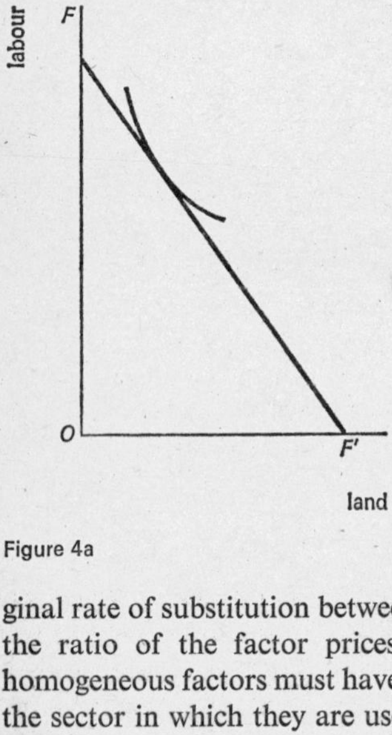

Figure 4a

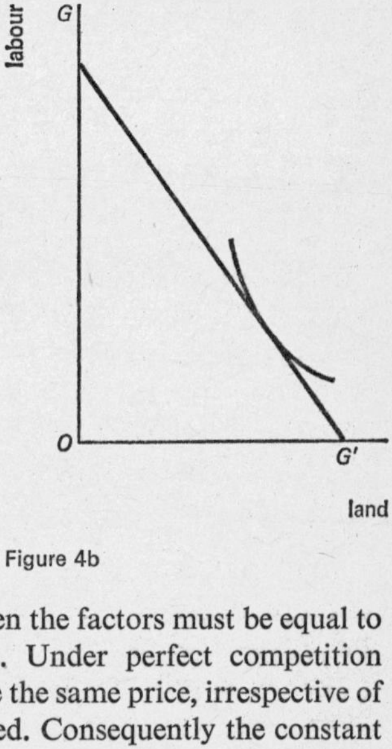

Figure 4b

ginal rate of substitution between the factors must be equal to the ratio of the factor prices. Under perfect competition homogeneous factors must have the same price, irrespective of the sector in which they are used. Consequently the constant factor outlay lines must have the same slope, as in Figures 4a and b, so that the marginal rates of substitution between land and labour must be the same in sectors A and B. Hence, under perfect competition, production will always take place on the boundary of the transformation curve as the crucial efficiency condition will always be satisfied.

We now go on to the question of which point on the transformation curve will be the one at which production will take place. Obviously, the answer will depend on the relative prices of the two goods A and B. Suppose that the prices of these goods are £2 per unit of A and £6 per unit of B. Producers will then only be in equilibrium if the resources that they use to produce one unit of B are just sufficient to produce three units of A. For if these resources can produce say 4A it will be profitable to divert resources from B to A, losing £6 on the one unit of B but gaining £8 on the four units of A. On the other hand if these resources can produce say 2A then it will be profitable to switch from A to B, losing £4 on the two units of A but gaining £6 on the one unit of B. In other words equilibrium requires that the marginal rate of transformation between A and B is three units of A for one unit of B, equal to the ratio of their prices. This condition must of course hold for any given price-ratio.

The price-ratio between A and B could be represented by the slope of a family of negatively inclined straight lines in Figure 1. The point on the transformation curve at which it is tangential to one of these lines will indicate the equilibrium quantities of A and B that will be supplied since this corresponds to the condition that the marginal rate of transformation is equal to the price-ratio. As the price-ratio is raised in favour of A the lines would become steeper, and the tangency point would move in the direction of larger quantities of A being supplied and smaller quantities of B.

In Figure 5 let the ratio of the price of A to the price of B be measured along the vertical axis, the supply of A along OX and the supply of B along OX'. For low values of this ratio the supply of A will be zero since the tangency would be at the point T in Figure 1 where the maximum amount of B is produced but no A. As the price-ratio is raised the supply of A will rise and of B will fall until the supply of B becomes zero and that of A reaches its maximum. The supply curve of A will therefore be *Oab* and the supply curve of B will be *cde* in Figure 5. For price-ratios higher than *Oe* the supply curve of B will coincide with the vertical axis OY whereas the supply curve of A will be the vertical continuation of *Oab*.

We have therefore shown that for any given price-ratio a unique point on the transformation curve is determined, and hence the quantities supplied of A and B can be read off Figure 5. But to every point on the transformation curve there corresponds a unique point on the efficiency locus of the box diagram, and hence an allocation of the factors to the two sectors. The marginal product of each factor, and hence its price in real terms under conditions of perfect competition, will thus be determined. If the distribution of the factors supplied over the individual households in the economy is taken as given, the real

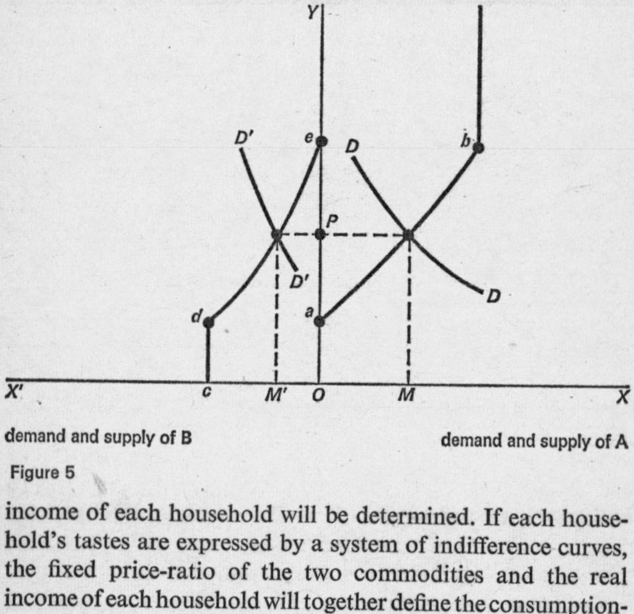

Figure 5

income of each household will be determined. If each household's tastes are expressed by a system of indifference curves, the fixed price-ratio of the two commodities and the real income of each household will together define the consumption-possibilities locus for each of the households as a negatively sloped line on an indifference curve diagram, and the equilibrium quantities of A and B demanded will be determined by the point of tangency between the consumption-possibilities line and an indifference curve. The quantities demanded by each household at a given price-ratio can then be summed to obtain the aggregate demand for each commodity at the price-ratio. Changing the price-ratio will change the commodity supplies, factor allocations and factor incomes, but for each price-ratio the factor incomes, and hence the quantities of A and B demanded, are determinate so that we can draw demand curves DD for A and $D'D'$ for B. It should be emphasized that these demand curves are different from the usual concept of a demand curve which assumes incomes to be fixed all along the curve. In the constructions used here the incomes of the factors are varying from point to point, the marginal productivities of the factors changing in response to the re-allocation induced by the change in the commodity price-ratio. The demand curves however are drawn with the usual property of the quantity demanded falling as the price rises, the possibility of income changes acting sufficiently powerfully in the opposite direction being excluded. This assumption has the important consequence of making the final equilibrium unique.

Assuming constant returns to scale we have the following conditions holding:

$$\text{MPP}(L_A) \times L_A + \text{MPP}(T_A) \times T_A = A^S \qquad \mathbf{1}$$

$$\text{MPP}(L_B) \times L_B + \text{MPP}(T_B) \times T_B = B^S \qquad \mathbf{2}$$

where MPP stands for marginal physical productivity, L_A and L_B for the labour used in A and B, T_A and T_B for the land used in A and B and A^S and B^S for the amounts of A and B supplied. The relations **1** and **2** therefore imply that when each factor is paid its marginal product the total product is exhausted. Multiplying **1** by P_A and **2** by P_B and then adding we have:

$$w(L_A + L_B) + r(T_A + T_B) = P_A A^S + P_B B^S \qquad \mathbf{3}$$

since P_A MPP(L_A) = P_B MPP(L_B) = w, the money wage-rate and P_A MPP(T_A) = P_B MPP(T_B) = r, the money rental of land. In other words **3** tells us that total factor incomes are equal to the value of total production supplied. Since we are given only the ratio of prices, one of them, say P_B, is arbitrary and may be put equal to unity.

Since it is assumed that households spend all their income on one or the other of the two commodities we have

$$P_A A^D + P_B B^D = w(L_A + L_B) + r(T_A + T_B) \qquad \mathbf{4}$$

where A^D and B^D stand for amounts demanded. From **3** and **4** it now follows that

$$P_A A^D + P_B B^D = P_A A^S + P_B B^S. \qquad \mathbf{5}$$

If at a certain price-ratio $OP = P_A^*/P_B^*$ we have the demand for A equal to the supply

$$A^D = A^S \qquad \mathbf{6}$$

we can multiply both sides by P_A^* and subtract from **5**, which holds for any values of P_A and P_B, to obtain

$$P_B^* B^D = P_B^* B^S$$

so that

$$B^D = B^S \qquad \mathbf{7}$$

at the price-ratio $OP = P_A^*/P_B^*$. In other words equilibrium in one market at a given price-ratio implies equilibrium in the other market at the same price-ratio. OM and OM' denote the equilibrium outputs of A and B in Figure 5. This means that the equilibrium point on the transformation curve is determined and therefore the factor allocations and marginal productivities and hence factor prices can be determined by the corresponding point on the efficiency-locus. The general equilibrium of the whole economy has therefore been established.

International Equilibrium and the Terms of Trade

We shall now go on to show how the general equilibrium analysis of the last section can be extended to cover international trade between the home country and the 'rest of the world' treated as a single entity. The assumption of perfect competition continues, both internally for each of the trading partners and also for the transactions between them. Thus not only are monopolistic private firms excluded but also government action such as tariffs and quotas designed to increase national benefit from trade at the expense of the foreigner. Citizens of each country take the prices at which they can export or import as given and adjust their behaviour accordingly. We shall also assume that transport costs are zero.

If there is no trade between them both the home country and the 'rest of the world' will each be in the type of domestic equilibrium described by Figure 5. The same factors of production are assumed to be used in both countries and the same commodities produced but since factor endowments, technology and tastes may all differ the price-ratio at which equilibrium is achieved will not be the same in each country, except by accident. Let us suppose that the equilibrium price-ratio in 'the rest of the world' is *OR* and that *OR* is greater than *OP*, that is, the price of A relative to the price of B is lower in the home country than abroad.

Suppose that the international price-ratio, which citizens of both countries take as given, is *OR*. At this price-ratio foreigners will not want to export or import as their domestic demands and supplies are in balance. But the home country will have an excess supply of A and an excess demand for B, which means that the combined world market will have a surplus of A and a shortage of B. This will cause the world price of A to fall relative to the world price of B. The international price-ratio cannot, however, fall all the way to *OP* since then the home country will be in balance for both commodities but the 'rest of the world' will have an excess demand for A and an excess supply of B. At some intermediate price-ratio between *OP* and *OR* the home country's excess supply of A will be exactly matched by the 'rest of the world's' excess demand for A and the home country's excess demand for B will be exactly matched by the excess supply from the 'rest of the world'. Thus international equilibrium will be achieved at a price-ratio intermediate between *OP* and *OR*, with the home country exporting A and importing B while the 'rest of the world' exports B and imports A.

We need to prove that just as in the case of the single country equilibrium of Figure 5 the price-ratio which equates demand and supply in one market must necessarily equate it in the other. We have for each country the condition that the total value of supplies equals the total value of demands:

$$P_A A_H^D + P_B B_H^D = P_A A_H^S + P_B B_H^S \qquad 1$$

$$P_A A_F^D + P_B B_F^D = P_A A_F^S + P_B B_F^S \qquad 2$$

where the subscripts H and F refer to home and foreign respectively. Adding **1** and **2** together we obtain

$$P_A(A_H^D + A_F^D) + P_B(B_H^D + B_F^D) = P_A(A_H^S + A_F^S) + P_B(B_H^S + B_F^S). \qquad 3$$

If, at a particular price-ratio, the market for A is in equilibrium we would have

$$(A_H^D + A_F^D) = (A_H^S + A_F^S). \qquad 4$$

Multiplying both sides by P_A, suptracting from **3** and then dividing the result by P_B gives

$$(B_H^D + B_F^D) = (B_H^S + B_F^S), \qquad 5$$

which was to be proved.

From **4** and **5** also follow

$$A_H^D - A_H^S = A_F^S - A_F^D \qquad 6$$

$$B_H^D - B_H^S = B_F^S - B_F^D \qquad 7$$

which state that one country's net export (import) of a commodity is equal to the other country's net import (export). Conditions **1** and **2** ensure that neither country can be a net exporter or importer of both commodities. We have already seen that the home country will export A while the 'rest of the world' exports B.

The equilibrium of international trade could be graphically depicted by a diagram analogous to Figure 5 but with the national demand and supply curves for each commodity replaced in each case by aggregate curves obtained by lateral summation of the two individual country curves. The equilibrium international price-ratio or *terms of trade* would be determined by the intersection of these combined demand and supply curves, and the quantities of each commodity exported or imported determined by the difference between national supply and demand at this price-ratio.

The equilibrium situation in each commodity market can be illustrated by the back-to-back diagram of Figure 6. Let *SS* and *DD* in the right-hand side of the diagram represent the supply and demand curves for A in the home country and *S'S'* and *D'D'* in the left-hand side the corresponding curves for the rest of the world. The equilibrium price-ratios for each country in isolation are *OP* and *OR*. The equilibrium terms of trade is *OQ* at which the excess supply of A in the home country is

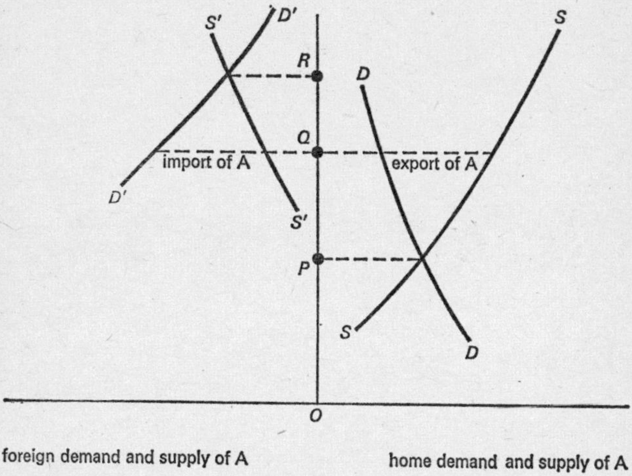

Figure 6

exactly equal to the excess demand for A in the 'rest of the world'. This difference between the two curves at the equilibrium terms of trade represents the export of A by the home country and the import of A by the rest of the world. A similar diagram could be drawn for commodity B to show the export of B from the 'rest of the world' and the import of B by the home country at the terms of trade *OQ*.

We have seen that the pattern of trade is for the home country to export A and import B. Why is this? In isolation, the price of A relative to the price of B, and hence the marginal rate of transformation between A and B, is lower in the home country.

Let us say that *OP* is two units of B per unit of A and that *OR* is five units of B per unit of A. This means that the marginal opportunity cost of 1A is two units of B at home but five units of B abroad. Hence in real terms, A is cheaper at home than abroad. This is why it is exported. On the other hand these same figures imply that the marginal opportunity cost of one unit of B at home is half a unit of A whereas abroad it is one fifth of a unit of A. This makes B cheaper abroad in real terms and hence it is imported by the home country. This is the famous principle of 'comparative cost', or 'comparative advantage', which states that a country will export the commodity which it can produce at a lower comparative cost, or, saying the same thing in another way, in which it has the greater comparative advantage in production. After trade is opened up, however, a common equilibrium price-ratio is established and so the opportunity costs of A will be the same in the two countries. Increased production of A at home will lead to a rise in its opportunity cost while abroad the opportunity cost of B will rise until the cost of each commodity is the same at the margin in both countries. The principle of comparative costs was discovered by Torrens and Ricardo. The explicit determination of the equilibrium terms of trade, however, was accomplished only by John Stuart Mill and Alfred Marshall, who introduced the famous technique of 'offer curves' for this purpose.

Although we have used a general equilibrium version of demand and supply analysis to determine the equilibrium terms of trade and export-import volumes instead of the traditional Marshallian technique the relationship between them is easily explained. In Figure 7 the export and import of A by the home country is measured along the horizontal axis and the export and import of B along the vertical. The slope of a straight line through the origin measures the rate at which A and B can be exchanged against each other. Thus the slope of this line corresponds to a point on the vertical axis of Figure 5 along which the price-ratio is measured. The amount of A and B that will be exported or imported at a given price-ratio can be read off Figure 5 and plotted on Figure 7. As the price-ratio is varied the straight line through the origin in Figure 7 will be rotated, tracing out the curve *COC′*. This is the Marshallian offer curve of the home country. The slope of a straight line from the origin to a point on the offer curve measures the terms of trade and the co-ordinates of that point measure either the export of A and import of B, as in the upper right-hand quadrant, or the export of B and import of A, as in the lower left-hand quadrant. The Marshallian offer curve of Figure 7 can thus be derived directly from Figure 5 whereas the reverse is not the case. Figure 5 is the more basic construction since it shows not only exports and imports but production and consumption as well. *ROR′* represents the offer curve of the 'rest of the world', constructed in a similar manner to *COC′* but turned upside down so that export of A by the home country will coincide with import of B by the 'rest of the world' and vice versa. At terms of trade equal to the slope of the straight line *OQ*, where the two offer curves intersect, the export of A by the home country is exactly matched by the import of A by the 'rest of the world' and the export of B by the latter is exactly matched by imports into the home country. *OQ* is therefore the equilibrium terms of trade and *OM* and *ON* are the equilibrium amounts of A and B entering into international trade.

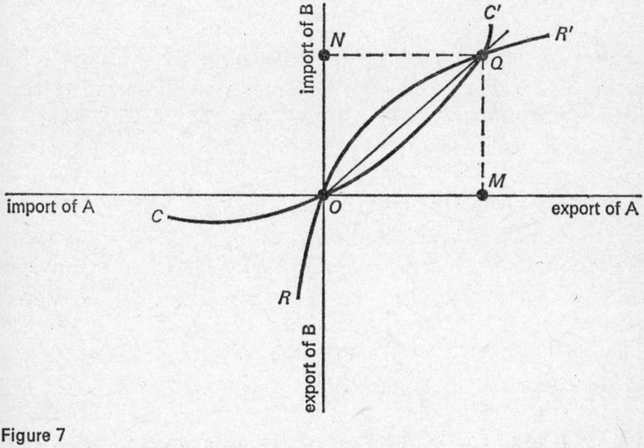

Figure 7

The analysis has so far been conducted on the assumption that the 'rest of the world' can be treated as if it were a single country. Although the two-country model has an honourable tradition going back all the way to Ricardo it is clearly desirable to extend the analysis to cover any number of countries. This can be done quite easily with the general equilibrium version of demand and supply that we have used for the two-country model. If there are *n* countries then there will be *n* transformation curves with their corresponding box diagrams and *n* pairs of demand curves (one each for the two goods in the *n* countries). To each value of the price-ratio for the two goods, which must be the same in all countries with perfect competition and the absence of transport costs and tariffs, there will correspond a supply and demand for A and B in each country determined in the manner described already. These demand and supply curves can be aggregated by lateral summation in the usual manner and world demand and supply curves derived for each commodity just as before, but without any limitation on the number of countries. The price-ratio at which international equilibrium is determined will be at the intersection point of these world curves. At this price-ratio some countries will be exporters of A and others of B. The outcome for each country will be determined by whether there is an excess supply or excess demand for A at home at the international equilibrium price-ratio. The exports and imports of each country can be read off the individual demand and supply diagrams, given the equilibrium price-ratio.

An alternative route to the same solution would be first to aggregate the individual transformation curves into a single world transformation curve and then to derive the world supply curves for A and B from this curve. At each price-ratio the world supply of A and B is equal to the sum of the amounts supplied in each country determined by the condition that the marginal rate of transformation between A and B is equal to the price-ratio. Since the price-ratio is the same for all countries the marginal rate of transformation must be the same in all countries for any level of world supply of A and B. This provides the clue to how the individual transformation curves are to be aggregated. If two curves are to be combined turn one diagram upside down, keeping the axes parallel, and slide one curve along the other in the manner described in Figure 8. The origin of the inverted diagram will then trace out the world transformation curve since at each point of tangency of the individual curves the marginal rates of transformation in the two countries will be equal. For three or more countries the additional curves can go on being added one at a time in the same manner and the world transformation curve built up successively.

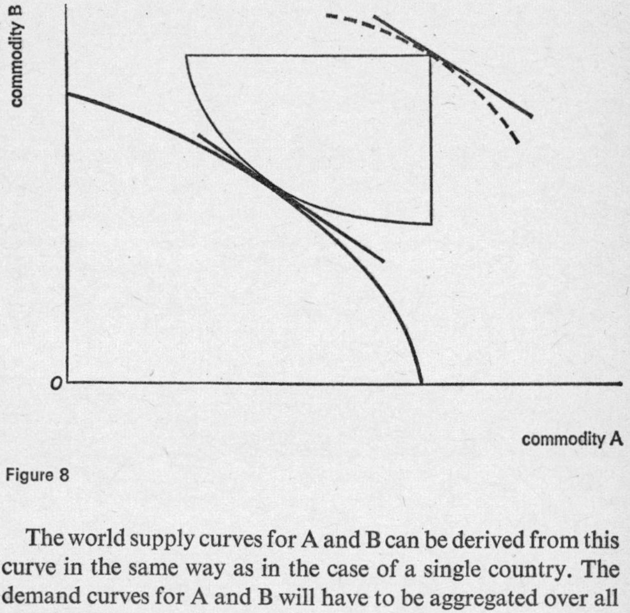

Figure 8

The world supply curves for A and B can be derived from this curve in the same way as in the case of a single country. The demand curves for A and B will have to be aggregated over all individual households in all countries as before.

Yet another alternative approach to the determination of multi-country equilibrium is through the offer curve. It was thought for a long time that the offer curve analysis was necessarily limited to the case of only two countries, but in 1952, G. S. Becker showed that there is a very simple technique for the combination of any number of offer curves (Becker, 1952). The amount that a country is willing to export and import at a given price-ratio is marked by a point on a straight line through the origin of the offer curve diagram, such as the one in Figure 7. The amount that several countries are willing to export and import at this price-ratio can be marked by a point, on the same straight line, which represents the combined volume of exports and imports of all countries. For each price-ratio the total exports and imports can be determined in this manner and a multi-country offer curve accordingly built up.

If it is known which countries will export A and which B in the final equilibrium then the offer curves of A exporters can be integrated into one combined curve and similarly for B exporters. The determination of the world equilibrium price-ratio and export-import volumes can be depicted by the intersection of these composite offer curves.

The offer curve technique for the analysis of multi-country equilibrium has the defect that one of the properties of the equilibrium solution, the question of which countries export which good, must be known for the technique to be applied. This is not necessary with the more straightforward supply and demand approach, where countries do not have to be divided into A and B exporters before the appropriate curves are aggregated.

Finally it should be pointed out that all versions of the multi-country model only tell us how much the total export or import of each good by each country will be. The geographical pattern of the *direction* of trade, the destinations of exports and the sources of imports are not determinate. World trade is treated as though all transactions go through some central clearing market with no direct link between buyers and sellers. This is one of the consequences of the assumption that there are no transport costs.

The analysis of trade with more than two commodities will be dealt with in chapter 3, within the specific Ricardian and Heckscher-Ohlin frameworks. A full mathematical analysis of international trade with any number of countries and commodities is given in a well-known work by J. L. Mosak (1944).

3 The Determinants of International Specialization I

In the previous chapter we have seen how the equilibrium terms and volume of trade are determined, given the factor endowments, technology and tastes in the individual countries. In particular, it was shown that each country exports the commodity that it can produce at a lower marginal opportunity cost in the absence of trade. In the post-trade equilibrium, of course, the marginal opportunity cost of production for each commodity will be the same in both countries since a common price-ratio is established.

The traditional answer to the question of why a particular country exports a particular commodity is simply that it is because it can produce it, as we have shown in the last chapter, at a lower comparative cost. It is desirable, however, to go deeper, and to inquire why it is that the patterns of comparative costs should be as they are. Obviously if countries were identical in every respect then, in the absence of the opportunity to trade, the domestic equilibrium price-ratios, and hence comparative cost-ratios, would be the same everywhere and there will be no incentive to trade even if the opportunity to do so became available. Hence the fundamental causes of international specialization and trade must be sought in *differences* between countries which, if universal perfect competition and the absence of transport costs is assumed, means differences in factor endowments, technology or tastes. Much of the literature of the last two decades has been concerned with the attempt to isolate logically, and also to examine empirically, the effects of each of these differences on the structure of trade. The present chapter will examine systematically the consequences for trade of each of these differences in turn.

Differences in Scale

Suppose that the two countries have exactly the same constant-returns-to-scale technologies for the production of each of the two goods A and B and also the same over-all ratio of land to labour. Hence as far as production is concerned the countries differ only in scale. The shapes of the box diagrams and transformation curves will be exactly the same. In Figure 9 let *TT* and *T′T′* denote the transformation curves of the two countries. Since the only difference is in scale the slopes of *TT* and *T′T′* will be the same along any ray through the origin, such as *OPP′* in Figure 9.

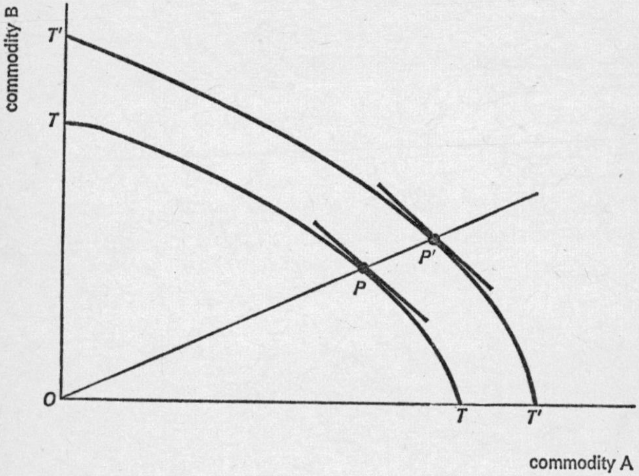

Figure 9

Let us further suppose that the pattern of tastes is also identical in the two countries in the sense that at the same price-ratio and real income (measured in terms of either good) the amounts of the two goods consumed in each country would be the same. Then, if *P* is the equilibrium point for the smaller country in the absence of trade, could we say that *P′* must be the corresponding point for the larger country? If this were so no trade would take place if the countries were brought into contact with each other since the price-ratio and hence comparative cost-ratios would be the same. It is readily seen, however, that there is no reason for P' to be the equilibrium point for the larger country unless the *further* assumption is made that the income-elasticities of demand for the two goods are equal to unity, i.e. the same proportion of the two goods is demanded at the same price-ratio, regardless of the level of real income. If the income-elasticity of demand for A is greater than unity (and hence less than unity for B) there will be excess demand for A and excess supply of B at the point P', causing the equilibrium point on $T'T'$ to be somewhere to the right of P' with a larger production of A and a smaller production of B. Hence, in the absence of trade, the relative price of A will be higher in the larger country and therefore also its comparative cost of producing A. Hence if trade is opened, the smaller country will export A to the larger country and import B in return.

Two conclusions worth noting follow from our analysis. First, it is *not* true that if two countries have identical tastes, technology and factor endowment proportions that there will be no trade between them. This will only be true if the identical taste patterns are such that for every possible price-ratio the income-elasticities are equal to unity. In other words difference in scale alone can be a sufficient cause for trade. The next conclusion tells us something about the pattern of trade that will arise if countries differ only in scale. Commodities for which the income-elasticity of demand is greater than unity will be exported by the smaller countries, and those for which the income-elasticity of demand is less than unity will be exported by the larger countries. It should be remembered, however, that the income-elasticities refer to national aggregates and not to individual household demand behaviour.

Differences in Tastes

If the two countries have identical amounts of both factors and also identical technologies for each of the goods then their respective transformation curves will also be identical. Differences in tastes, which lead to different equilibrium points on the identical transformation curves in the absence of trade, will therefore be the only possible cause of differences in comparative costs. Countries will import the goods for which their comparative preference in consumption is greater since in the absence of trade the comparative costs of these goods will be higher at home than abroad.

Differences in Factor Endowments

In this section we shall compare the structure of production in the two countries, assuming the same constant returns to scale technology for each good in both countries, but with different factor endowments. The pattern of tastes in both countries will be taken not only as identical but as being of the special type where income-elasticities are unity for all price-ratios. This makes the proportions in which goods are demanded independent of the level of income and hence independent of scale. On these assumptions we shall try to formulate some propositions about the influence of factor endowment on the structure of international trade.

We begin by establishing a very important relationship between commodity price-ratios and factor price-ratios. Suppose that the relative price of commodities A and B is given. Obviously, this will influence the price-ratio of the two factors that we call labour and land. But what will be the nature of this influence? In particular, could we say that one and only one factor price-ratio corresponds to any given commodity price-ratio? With the assumption of perfect competition it follows that if the commodity price-ratio is, say, three units of A for one unit of B, and if both commodities are produced, then the factor cost of producing three units of A must be equal to that for producing one unit of B. In Figure 10 we depict the constant factor cost line *FF* (along which the total expenditure on the two factors is constant) as being tangential to both the isoquant for three units of A and the isoquant for one unit of B. Since constant returns to scale for both commodities is assumed the absolute levels of production are not relevant at all. The slope of *FF*, which is the factor price-ratio, is therefore determined by the commodity price-ratio of three units for A for one unit of B. If the commodity price-ratio were to change, for example to 4A for 1B, the effect on the factor price-ratio could be determined by finding the slope of a common tangent to the isoquants for four units of A and one unit of B.

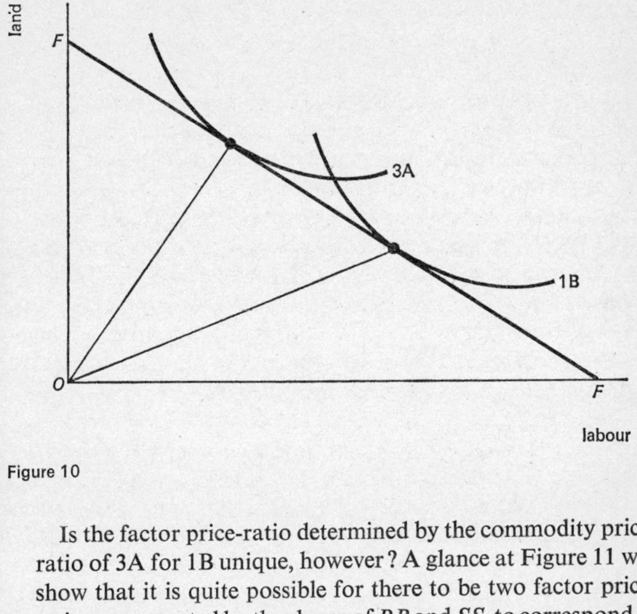

Figure 10

Is the factor price-ratio determined by the commodity price-ratio of 3A for 1B unique, however? A glance at Figure 11 will show that it is quite possible for there to be two factor price-ratios, represented by the slopes of *RR* and *SS*, to correspond to the same commodity price-ratio of 3A for 1B. Hence, in order for a commodity price-ratio to determine *uniquely* a factor price-ratio when both commodities are being produced under perfectly competitive conditions, as is assumed here, it is necessary to rule out cases such as that of Figure 11. This can be done by the assumption that the technologies for the two goods are such that at *any* factor price-ratio the land-labour ratio in the production of one of the goods is higher than in the other. This condition is readily seen to be incompatible with the case of Figure 11 since at the factor price-ratio corresponding to *RR* the land-labour ratio is higher in A production, whereas at that corresponding to *SS* the land-labour ratio is higher in B production. Geometrically, this conditon amounts to the requirement that the isoquants for 3A and 1B (or for whatever magnitudes correspond to the given price-ratio) must

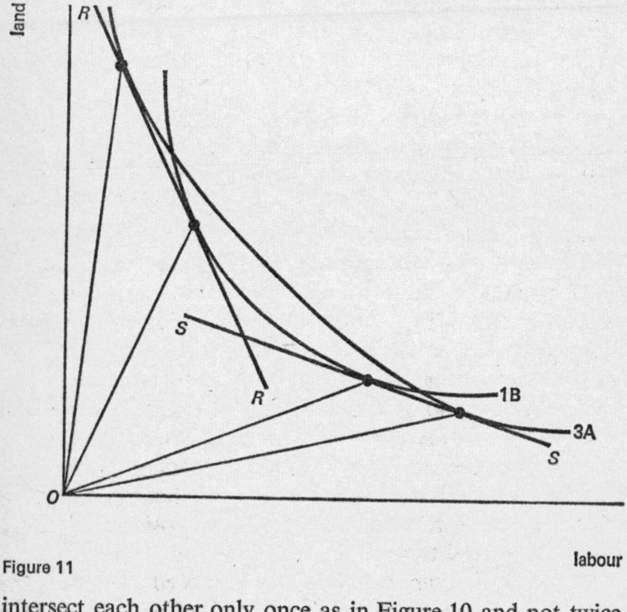

Figure 11

intersect each other only once as in Figure 10 and not twice as in Figure 11, or more times. If this condition is met we can unambigiously define A as the 'land-intensive' commodity and B as the 'labour-intensive' commodity.

Under the 'strong' factor-intensity assumption (i.e. that A is always land-intensive and B labour-intensive) we can also establish the result that the higher the relative price of a commodity the higher must be the relative price of the factor which is used more intensively in its production. To see this suppose that the commodity price-ratio is 4A for 1B in Figure 10 instead of 3A for 1B. Then it is easy to see that the slope of the common tangent to the isoquants for 4A and 1B would be steeper, the land-labour ratio rising in the production of both commodities, implying that the price of labour has risen relative to the price of land. Since it is B, the labour-intensive commodity, that now has the more favourable price-ratio, our contention is proved. Thus we have established the factor price-ratio as uniquely determined by the commodity price-ratio, and also that the factor price-ratio changes in favour of the factor used intensively in the commodity in favour of which the relative commodity price is changing.

In view of its importance it would be useful to give a simple economic interpretation of why this result holds. Suppose 3A was worth 1B but now 4A is worth 1B. Perfect competition requires that the same absolute factor prices prevail in production of both A and B. If relative factor prices are unchanged cost minimization and constant returns to scale imply that 4A will cost one and a third as much as 1B whereas by hypothesis the cost of 4A and 1B is the same. A factor price shift in favour of land will make the cost of 4A even greater than that of $1\frac{1}{3}$B since the proportion of land cost to total cost is greater for the land-intensive commodity A. Thus the only behaviour of relative factor prices consistent with the conditions assumed is for the price of labour to rise relative to the price of land. In this case the cost of 1B will rise relatively more than the cost of the 3A, because it is relatively more labour-intensive. This makes it possible for 1B to be worth 4A as required.

If one of the commodities is not produced at all, then the analysis no longer applies since the cost of producing it can exceed the cost of producing the commodity that is produced by any amount. In other words the factor prices will not be determined by the common tangent since there is no necessity for costs to be equalized if one of the commodities is not produced.

The analysis that we have presented was originally developed by Lerner to prove that, under the assumptions made about production conditions, it follows that free trade must equalize factor prices between countries if technology is identical, and there are no transport costs (Lerner, 1952). This is because free trade will equalize the commodity price-ratio in the two countries and, with identical constant returns to scale technology and the 'strong' factor-intensity assumption, a unique factor price-ratio is determined. With constant returns to scale the marginal productivities of factors depend only on the ratios in which they are combined, and since these are uniquely determined as a result of the 'strong' factor-intensity assumption it follows that the absolute levels of the factor prices must also be equal and not just their ratio. Under the name of the 'factor price equalization theorem', also discovered independently by Samuelson, this remarkable result has stirred up a lot of controversy and further research in the last twenty years. We shall not pursue the matter further except in connexion with the determinants of international specialization.

Suppose that commodity A is land-intensive and commodity B labour-intensive in the sense defined above. Suppose further that one country is 'land-abundant' and the other 'labour abundant' in the sense that the over-all ratio of land to labour is higher in the former country, each of these factors being of the same quality in both countries. Under these circumstances a hypothesis about the structure of trade suggests itself immediately – that the land-abundant country will export the land-intensive commodity A and the labour-abundant country the labour-intensive commodity B. The commonsense reasoning that gives rise to this hypothesis is that land would be relatively cheap in the land-abundant country giving it a comparative advantage in the land-intensive commodity; whereas labour would be relatively cheap in the other country giving it a comparative advantage in the labour-intensive commodity. This is the famous Heckscher-Ohlin theory of international trade, developed first in the inter-war years by the two Swedish economists, but rigorously analysed and tested only during the last twenty years (Heckscher, 1949; Ohlin, 1933).

We now turn to a rigorous examination of the Heckscher-Ohlin proposition, pointing out the assumptions necessary for its logical validity. The empirical tests of the theory as an explanatory hypothesis about the nature of international trade flows are considered in a later chapter.

First we need to prove that, at the same commodity price-ratio, the proportion of the land-intensive commodity's output to that of the labour-intensive commodity's will be higher, the higher is the over-all land-labour ratio. Intuitively we can see that this must be so since at the same commodity price-ratio we know that the land-labour ratios in the production of each commodity are uniquely determined so that the only way in which the higher over-all land-labour ratio can be absorbed is by increasing the output of the land-intensive commodity relative to that of the labour-intensive commodity.

A more rigorous proof can now be given as in Figure 12. Supposing the factor endowments of two countries to be given, let *HIJK* represent the box diagram of the country that has the smaller absolute amount of land, with the origin of the A isoquants at *H* and of the B isoquants at *J*. The sides *HI* and *JK* can also be used to measure the amount of land in the other country but of course the scale will have to be changed. Thus if the second country has double the land of the first, one unit of length along *HI* or *JK* will represent twice the amount of land as for the first country. Similarly the sides *HK* and *IJ* can also be used to measure the amount of labour in the second country if the scale is suitably adjusted. If the over-all ratio of land to labour is the same in the two countries then *HIJK* could represent the box diagram of the second country as well, if technology exhibits constant returns to scale and is the same for both countries, the only difference being in the scale factor. Since a given commodity price-ratio uniquely determines the factor-price ratio and land-labour ratios in each good, let the slopes of *Ha* and *Ja* represent the land-labour ratios for commodities A and B respectively, A being land-intensive and B labour-intensive. Thus at the same commodity price-ratio the slopes of *Ha* and *Ja* will represent the land-labour ratios of A and B production in *both* countries. Since the only difference is the scale factor (which is the same for land and labour) the outputs of A and B will have the same proportion to each other in both countries.

If the land-labour ratio in the country with the larger absolute amount of land is smaller, *HIJK* can no longer represent the box diagram for both countries since the changes in scale required for the land and labour axes are no longer uniform. Suppose, for example, that land is twice as great but labour is three times as great in the second country. Then *HI* and *JK* can still measure the amount of land in the second country, with each unit of length now representing double the amount of land as before, but *IJ* and *HK* have each to be made 50 per cent longer in order to represent three times the amount of

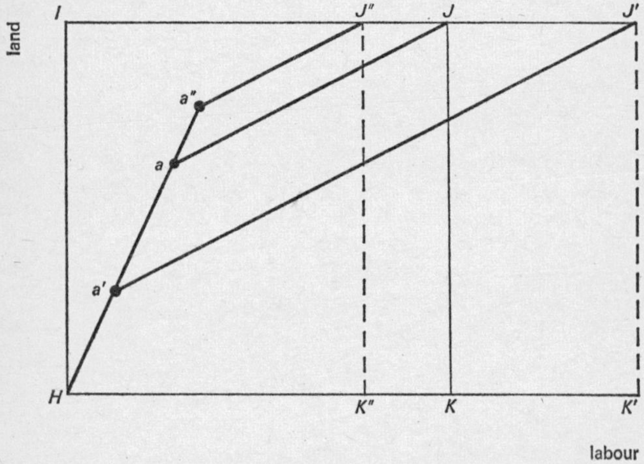

Figure 12

labour. Thus, if the land-labour ratio were smaller the box diagram of the second country would be like *HIJ′K′* in Figure 12. Similarly if the land-labour ratio were larger then the box diagram of the second country would be like *HIJ″K″*.

We can now find out what will happen to the proportion of A and B at the same commodity price-ratio as the over-all land-labour ratio is changed. Since the slopes of *Ha* and *Ja* represent the land-labour ratios for each good corresponding to the given commodity price-ratio these slopes must remain the same, whatever the over-all land-labour ratio may be. Since an A and a B isoquant are tangential at the point *a*, the points *a′* corresponding to $HIJ'K'$ and a'' corresponding to $HIJ''K''$ will also have A and B isoquants tangential to each other at them since the land-labour ratios for each good are the same at all these points. Hence each of them will lie on the efficiency locus of the corresponding box diagram. If land and labour increase in the same proportion we have the point a on $HJIK$ from which it follows that the proportion of A output to B output will be constant. If labour increases more than proportionately to land we have the point a' from which it follows that the proportion of A to B falls since $Ha'/J'a'$ is smaller than Ha/Ja. Similarly if labour increases proportionately less than land we have the point a'' from which it follows that the proportion of A to B has risen since $Ha''/J''a''$ is greater than Ha/Ja. These results mean that the output of the land-intensive good relative to that of the labour-intensive good varies directly with the over-all land-labour ratio when relative commodity prices are kept constant, as was to be proved.

Instead of this rather involved and tedious geometric proof a more succinct and elegant algebraic proof can be given. Let a_{11} and a_{21} denote the land and labour per unit of A output and a_{12} and a_{22} the land and labour per unit of B output. These coefficients will of course vary with the relative factor prices, but since a given commodity price-ratio uniquely determines a factor price-ratio these coefficients will be constants at the given commodity price-ratio. Denoting the total amounts of land and labour by M and L respectively we have:

$$a_{11}A + a_{12}B = M, \qquad 1$$

$$a_{21}A + a_{22}B = L.$$

These equations state that all the land and labour available are used in the production of the two goods. Dividing the equations by L we obtain

$$a_{11}\frac{A}{L} + a_{12}\frac{B}{L} = \frac{M}{L}, \qquad 3$$

$$a_{21}\frac{A}{L} + a_{22}\frac{B}{L} = 1. \qquad 4$$

Solving these equations for A/L and B/L yields

$$\frac{A}{L}=\frac{a_{22}M/L-a_{12}}{(a_{11}a_{22}-a_{21}a_{12})}, \qquad 5$$

$$\frac{B}{L}=\frac{a_{11}-a_{21}M/L}{(a_{11}a_{22}-a_{21}a_{12})}. \qquad 6$$

from which it follows that

$$\frac{A}{B}=\frac{a_{22}M/L-a_{12}}{a_{11}-a_{21}M/L}. \qquad 7$$

Equation **7** gives us the ratio of commodity outputs as a function of the land-labour ratio. The effect of variation in the land-labour ratio on the commodity ratio is obtained by differentiating **7** with respect to M/L yielding

$$\frac{d(A/B)}{d(M/L)}=\frac{(a_{11}a_{22}-a_{21}a_{12})}{(a_{11}-a_{21}M/L)^2}, \qquad 8$$

which indicates that

$$\frac{d(A/B)}{d(M/L)}\gtreqless 0,$$

according to whether

$$\frac{a_{11}}{a_{21}}\gtreqless\frac{a_{12}}{a_{22}},$$

that is, according as to whether A or B is the land-intensive commodity which is the result required to be proved.[1]

Suppose now that the home country has a higher land-labour ratio than the 'rest of the world'. Then at the same commodity price-ratio there will be a higher proportion of A output to B output (A being the land-intensive good) in the home country.

1. A special case of this result, when one factor is increased and the other held constant, is known as the Rybczynski theorem (see Rybczynski, 1955).

If the 'rest of the world's' demand and supply for A and B are in equilibrium at the given price-ratio in the absence of trade, the home country *cannot* be in equilibrium at the *same* commodity price-ratio in the absence of trade if the identical tastes at home and abroad are such that the same proportion of *A* and *B* is demanded, at any given price-ratio, regardless of income. This is because the home country will have a higher ratio of *A* to *B* in production at the same commodity price-ratio as the 'rest of the world', whereas she will demand the same ratio of *A* and *B*. There will therefore be an excess supply of A and an excess demand for B, lowering the price of A relative to the price of B until equilibrium is restored. Hence, in the absence of trade, the land-abundant home country will produce the land-intensive commodity relatively more cheaply than the 'rest of the world', which will produce the labour-intensive commodity relatively more cheaply. Hence the Heckscher-Ohlin theorem that each country will export the commodity which is intensive in the factor that it has in relative abundance is now proved.

If identity of tastes is defined less restrictively – A and B demanded in the same proportion at a given price ratio when incomes are the same, but income elasticities not unitary – it is possible that the land-abundant country will *import* the land-intensive good, as a result of a difference in real income levels. Thus, at the income level of the home country it may be that the proportion of *A* to *B* demanded at the same commodity price-ratio is *higher* than the ratio of *A* to *B* in production, which will cause A to be relatively more expensive at home in the absence of trade, thus resulting in the 'perverse' import of the land-intensive commodity into the land-abundant country.

Associated with the Heckscher-Ohlin model of international trade is the famous Stolper-Samuelson theorem that protection benefits the factor that is relatively scarce (Stolper and Samuelson, 1941). This theorem readily follows from the analysis already given. We have seen that with the hypothesis made about demand the land-abundant country will export the land-intensive good and import the labour-intensive one. Protection will reduce the price of the exported good relative to the imported good since the foreign demand for the former and the foreign supply of the latter is reduced. Since the commodity price-ratio moves in favour of the labour-intensive good, the relative factor price-ratio will move in favour of labour, the absolute level of the real wage-rate also rising, since the land-labour ratio will rise in the production of each commodity, raising the marginal productivity of labour in terms of either good.

Differences in Technology

In this section we shall examine the effects of international differences in technology on the pattern of specialization, assuming tastes and over-all factor proportions to be identical. It is obvious that, even with the same factor endowment, differences in technology will result in different shapes of the transformation curves so that identical tastes will still lead to differences in comparative costs and hence to trade. In order to obtain some clear-cut propositions, however, it is necessary to restrict the nature of the technological differences between countries to a type which is convenient to handle. This restriction is that the differences in technological efficiency between countries are 'neutral' with respect to the ratios in which the factors are combined. Thus suppose that one country can produce commodity A twice as efficiently as another. This will be taken to mean that the isoquant for two units of A in the more efficient country will exactly coincide with the isoquant for one unit of A in the less efficient country, if they are drawn with reference to the same co-ordinate axes. Thus the shapes of isoquants for the same commodity will be identical between countries but the numbers attached to them will differ for the same combinations of factors.

We shall now show in terms of our two-factor, two-good model that if over-all factor proportions are the same and that if the identical demand conditions are such that income-elasticities are unity for all price-ratios, there will be no trade if one country is *uniformly* more efficient in the production of both goods. To see this let us turn again to the box diagram *HIJK* in Figure 12. Since we are assuming the same over-all land-labour ratio *HIJK* can do double duty as the box diagram for both countries, with only the scales of the land and labour axes changed by a common factor. With 'neutral' technological differences for each of the goods the isoquants inside the box also need not be changed except for scale (the change in scale here however will in general be different from that for the sides of the box). If the point *a* gives us the production of A and B in one country for a given commodity price-ratio, it will also give us the production of A and B at the same commodity price-ratio in the other country. This is because the same commodity price-ratio will still correspond to the same factor price-ratio if the neutral technological difference is uniform for both goods. In Figure 10 the commodity price-ratio of 3A for 1B will still correspond to the factor price-ratio given by the slope of *FF* if efficiency is changed uniformly for both goods, since only the scale of the diagram has to be adjusted. The point *a* will therefore correspond to the same commodity price-ratio in the second country as well, since the factor price-ratio at *a* is unchanged. Suppose, for example, that the land and labour endowments of the second country are double those of the first, and that technological efficiency is 50 per cent greater for both goods. Then the production of A and B at the point *a* for the second country will both be three times as much as for the first (twice as great on account of double the factor endowment plus 50 per cent of that for greater efficiency). The ratio of A to B will therefore be the same in the two countries at the same price-ratio. Thus if one country is in equilibrium at the given price-ratio in the absence of trade, the other one will be also – with the special demand conditions assumed. Hence greater technological efficiency cannot be the cause of trade if the relative difference is the same for both goods. Trade can take place, however, if the unitary income elasticities for all price-ratios restriction are not met.

We now consider the case where the relative efficiency differences are not uniform between sectors. Intuition of course tells us that under these conditions a country will export the commodity in which its relative technological efficiency is greatest. A formal proof can be constructed as follows. We first observe that, when technological differences are not uniform, the same factor price-ratio does not correspond to the same commodity price-ratio as before. Thus suppose that one country is twice as efficient as the other in producing A and 50 per cent more efficient in producing B. Then if the isoquants tangential to *FF* in Figure 10 are 3A and 1B for the first country, they will be 6A and 1½B for the second country. Hence the factor price-ratio given by the slope of *FF* now corresponds to a commodity price-ratio of 4A for 1B in the second country as well as to 3A for 1B in the first country. It should be noted that the commodity price-ratio shifts in favour of the commodity in which the relative efficiency is *less*, at the same factor price-ratio. Alternatively, we can ascertain the shift in the factor price-ratio that takes place if the commodity price-ratio is kept unchanged. In Figure 10 the commodity price-ratio will be 3A for 1B in the first country and 6A for 1½B in the second, these being the different numbers attached to the isoquants in the two countries. If the commodity price-ratio is also to be 3A for 1B in the second country, this could be indicated by drawing the 4½A isoquant for the second country, and the common tangent to this isoquant and that for 1½B. At the same commodity price-ratio of 3A for 1B in both countries it will be seen that the land-labour ratio will be lower in the production of both commodities in the second country, so that the factor price-ratio shifts in favour of land. Thus the country that is relatively more efficient in producing the land-intensive commodity (which is what A is) will have a higher price of land relative to the price of labour.

We now go back to the box diagram *HIJK* of Figure 12, fortunately for the last time. Suppose that the home country is more efficient than abroad in both A and B but that she is relatively more efficient in A. The land-labour ratio is the same for both countries. At the point *a* the factor price-ratios will be the same for both countries since the efficiency differences are assumed to be neutral. The point *a* will therefore be on the efficiency-locus of the box diagrams for both countries. Since the home country is relatively more efficient in A, in a factor-neutral way, the ratio of A production to B production will be higher at home than abroad at the point *a*, that is to say at the same factor price-ratio. From the result established earlier we know that at the same factor price-ratio the commodity price-ratio will move in favour of the commodity in which the relative efficiency is less, which in this case is commodity B. We now wish to find out what will be the relative proportions of A and B production at the same commodity price-ratio in the two countries.

We have seen that at *a* the proportion of A production to B production will be higher than abroad. But at *a* the factor price-ratio is the same in the two countries so that, by the results obtained earlier, the ratio of the price of B to the price of A will be higher at home than abroad. At the same commodity price-ratio in the two countries we know that the land-labour ratio must fall in the production of both commodities at home, shifting relative factor prices in favour of land. For this to happen the production point must move to the right of *a* along the efficiency-locus of *HIJK*. The same result follows if we observe that the opportunity cost (equal to the commodity price-ratio) of B is higher in the home country at *a*, so that for it to be equal there must be less production of B since production takes place at increasing opportunity cost.

We have therefore proved that the home country will produce more A relative to B than abroad at the same commodity price-ratio. If demand conditions are such that the same proportions of A and B are demanded at the same price-ratio in both countries regardless of income, the home country will have an excess supply of A and an excess demand for B at the price-ratio that equilibrates demand and supply abroad in the absence of trade. Thus, the home country must have a lower price of A in terms of B to be in equilibrium. Hence she will have a comparative advantage in A, exporting this commodity and importing B if trade is opened. Commonsense intuition that a country will export the good that she can produce at greater relative efficiency is thus justified.

However, it should be noted that as in the case of the Heckscher-Ohlin theory, the special assumption about demand is required to rule out the possibility of a 'perverse' case. It is quite possible for the ratio of A to B demanded at the same price-ratio to be *higher* in the home country than the ratio of A to B produced even if tastes are identical in the two countries, because of a difference in income levels. In this case the price of A in terms of B will be higher in the home country in the absence of trade, and it will *import* the good that it can produce with the greater relative technological efficiency. This fact again serves as a reminder that comparative costs, or the marginal rate of transformation, depend on demand as well as technology and factor endowments and that inferences based on the last two variables alone will not always be correct.

The hypothesis that differences in relative technical efficiency are the cause of trade is linked with the name of Ricardo himself. In his original model labour is the only scarce factor in both countries and the input of this factor, required for each commodity, is a constant. With these assumptions the transformation curve of each country becomes a straight line. Denoting the labour inputs per unit of A and B in each country by a_1, a_2, b_1 and b_2 it is apparent that the slopes of the transformation curves will be equal to a_1/b_1 and a_2/b_2. These ratios define the pattern of comparative costs in the two countries. If $a_1/b_1 = a_2/b_2$ there will be no trade as the comparative costs are the same. This condition can be written as $a_1/a_2 = b_1/b_2$, that is, the greater technical efficiency of either one of the countries, if any, is uniform for both goods. If $a_1/b_1 < a_2 b_2$ implying that $a_1/a_2 < b_1/b_2$ then country 1 will export A since the labour input per unit of output is relatively lower for commodity A than for commodity B (i.e. technical efficiency is relatively greater in A than in B) in that country. Similarly if $a_1/b_1 > a_2 b_2$ so that $a_1/a_2 > b_1/b_2$ then country 1 will export B.

It is interesting to notice how the extreme simplicity of Ricardo's assumptions about production make comparative costs depend only upon technology. The amount of labour in each country only influences the scale of the transformation curve, leaving the slope unchanged. Demand conditions, which fix the equilibrium point on the curve in the absence of trade, are also irrelevant since the slope is constant all along the curve.

Hence we are left with differences in technology as the only possible cause of trade.

The Ricardian hypothesis can be extended, as above, into the context of a two-factor variable proportions model but then, as we have seen, factor endowments and demand conditions can shift the pattern of comparative advantage opposite to that indicated by technology alone.

One last result can be derived before we leave the subject of the influence of differences in technology. This is about the effect of trade (or protection if we look at the movement in the opposite direction) on factor prices. Trade will equalize the commodity price-ratio between countries but, as was shown earlier, this means that the factor price-ratios cannot be the same if the relative technological efficiencies are not uniformly different. With the Lerner diagram of Figure 10 we have seen that the land-labour ratio will be lower in the production of each commodity in the country that produces the land-intensive commodity with relatively greater efficiency than the labour-intensive commodity. Thus in Figure 10 the 3A isoquant will be pulled relatively lower than the 1B isoquant in a country that is relatively more efficient in the former commodity, making the common tangent to both isoquants flatter and reducing the land-labour ratio for both commodities; this implies that the price of land rises relative to the price of labour. Unlike the factor-price equalization that follows from the Heckscher-Ohlin model we have a situation where the price of the factor used intensively in the exported good is relatively higher than the price of the factor that is used intensively in the imported good, as compared with factor prices in the other country.

Trade will raise the relative price of the land-intensive good in the exporting country and it can again be shown by the Lerner diagram that this will raise the price of land and reduce the price of labour. In terms of Figure 10 a higher price of A relative to B, say 2A for 1B instead of 3A for 1B, is readily seen to imply a fall in the land-labour ratio for both commodities, and hence a rise in the price of land and a fall in the price of labour. Thus whether the export of a commodity which uses a certain factor intensively is due to factor endowments as on the Heckscher-Ohlin hypothesis, or technology as on the Ricardian hypothesis, the result is that trade will benefit that factor and consequently harm the factor used intensively in imports, since under constant returns to scale the marginal productivities of the two factors always move opposite to each other. The Stolper-Samuelson theorem therefore does not depend solely on the Heckscher-Ohlin hypothesis for its validity.

The Chain of Comparative Advantage

Our discussion in this chapter has so far been limited to the case of two countries and two commodities. In this section these restrictions will each be relaxed in turn but we shall not attempt a full analysis of many countries and commodities simultaneously.

We begin with many countries. There are three separate cases to consider, the Heckscher-Ohlin and the Ricardian with its two variants. It has been proved earlier that the higher the over-all land-labour ratio in a country the greater will be the proportion of the output of the land-intensive commodity at the same commodity price-ratio. Thus if we have *n* countries and rank them in terms of the land-labour ratio the same ranking will be obtained in terms of the ratio of A output to B output at a given price-ratio in each of them. If demand conditions depend only on relative prices and are identical for all countries, which as we have seen is a necessary assumption for the logical validity of the Heckscher-Ohlin theorem, then all countries will demand the same proportion of A and B at the same commodity price-ratio, regardless of their factor endowment. At commodity price-ratios very favourable to B the supply of A will be zero in all countries and there will be excess demand for A in all countries, that is there will be no country willing to export A. As, however, the commodity price-ratio is made more favourable to A, the supply of A will start to rise in all countries, and eventually there will be one country in which an excess supply of A will appear. It is easy to see that this must be the country with the highest land-labour ratio since the proportions in which A and B are demanded are the same for all countries, whereas the proportions in which they are supplied varies with the land-labour ratio. Further variation of the commodity price-ratio in favour of A will convert one country after another to having an excess supply of A, in the order of their land-labour ratios, until no country will eventually produce any B at all. International equilibrium must take place at some intermediate price-ratio at which the excess supplies of some countries exactly match the excess demands of the others.

From what has been said it is clear that the exporters of A will be at the higher end of the land-labour ratio scale while the importers of A and exporters of B will be at the lower end. If we say that the lower the price of A at which a country first exports A, the greater its comparative advantage in that commodity, then we can say that ranking countries according to the land-labour ratio corresponds exactly to ranking them in order of comparative advantage in A (which, read the opposite way, is of course the order of comparative advantage in B). Comparative advantage can thus be thought of as a *chain*, where the sequence of links is determined purely by factor endowments, demand conditions only determining the point where the chain is broken into one part containing the A exporters and, the other, the B exporters. Any exporter of A will be more land-abundant than any exporter of B so that the Heckscher-Ohlin theorem thus generalizes without difficulty to any number of countries.

The original Ricardian model with fixed labour inputs is now considered. Suppose that the ratio of labour inputs for A and B in the countries is such that

$$\frac{a_1}{b_1} < \frac{a_2}{b_2} < \ldots < \frac{a_n}{b_n},$$

that is, the countries are numbered such that the first country has the lowest opportunity cost for A, the second has the next lowest and so on. If the labour endowments in each country are given, a world transformation curve can easily be constructed as shown below in Figure 13. As more and more A production is desired, the switch from B production to A production takes place first in the country most efficient in A production among those not already completely specialized on this commodity.

Although only five countries are shown in Figure 13 the method is obviously applicable to any number of countries. Assuming again, for simplicity, identical demand patterns with unitary income-elasticities at all price-ratios we can determine

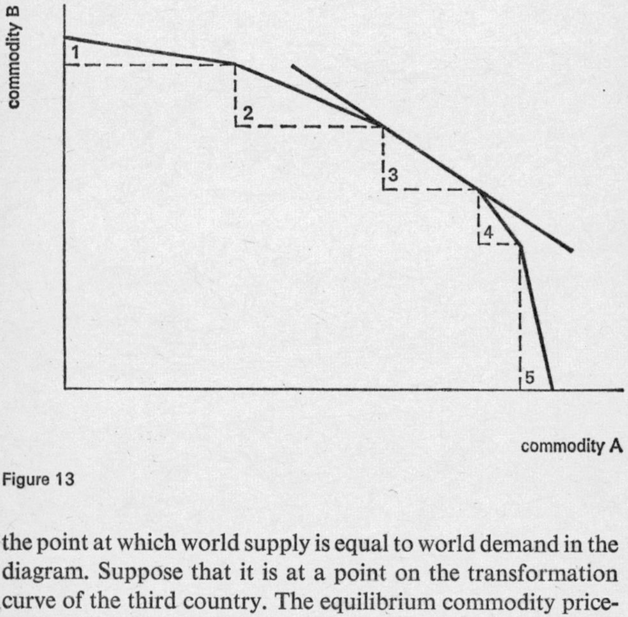

Figure 13

the point at which world supply is equal to world demand in the diagram. Suppose that it is at a point on the transformation curve of the third country. The equilibrium commodity price-ratio will then be determined by the slope of country 3's transformation curve. It is clear that countries 1 and 2 will specialize completely on A production, importing their requirements of B, while countries 4 and 5 will specialize completely on B and import their requirements of A. Country 3 will produce both commodities and in general may be either an A or a B exporter or may not engage in trade at all.

In this case also we have a 'chain of comparative advantage', this time determined by technological differences between the countries, with demand conditions serving only to 'break the chain' between A exporters and B exporters. The relative roles of demand and cost factors in international trade has been the subject of considerable controversy. The late Frank Graham of Princeton maintained that an exaggerated importance had been given to demand in the determination of the terms of trade since the time of Marshall, due, in his opinion, to the practice of working only with two-country, two-good models (Graham, 1948). In this case reciprocal demand is needed to determine the terms of trade within the range spanned by the cost ratios of the two countries, unless one country is very large relative to the other so that the terms of trade coincide with its own cost ratio. From Figure 13, however, it can be seen that in the multi-country case the terms of trade are almost certain to be equal to the cost ratio of some intermediate country in the chain of comparative advantage. Only if world equilibrium is at one of the points of discontinuity on the world transformation curve must demand be brought in to determine the exact terms of trade in between the cost ratios on either side. Although Graham must be given great credit for his pioneering explorations of multi-country and multi-commodity models, it appears that his criticism of the conventional theory on this question is misguided. The fact that the terms of trade will usually be equal to the cost ratio of some intermediate or 'marginal' country does not mean that demand can be dispensed with, for it is precisely the demand conditions that determine which is the marginal country whose cost ratio is equal to the terms of trade.

The final multi-country case to be examined is where there are neutral efficiency differences in production, factor endowment ratios being everywhere the same. In this case countries can be ranked in the order of relative efficiency in A production to B production. It has been proved earlier that the greater the relative efficiency in A production the higher will be the ratio of A output to B output for a given commodity price-ratio. With the special hypothesis about demand it is easy to prove in the same way as for the Heckscher-Ohlin case that there will be a chain of comparative advantage, with the country relatively most efficient in A at the top and the one relatively least efficient at the bottom, with demand conditions cutting the chain to separate the A exporters in the upper half from the B exporters in the lower.

We now turn to the consideration of many commodities and two countries, taking the Heckscher-Ohlin case first. It is assumed that the commodities can be ranked unambiguously in order of factor-intensity at any factor price-ratio. Commodity A is more land-intensive then commodity B, which in turn is more land-intensive than commodity C and so on. Under these conditions it can be proved that if A is relatively cheaper than B in one country, then B must be relatively cheaper than C and so on all down the line. There is again a chain of comparative advantage as in the multi-country, two-commodity case so that commodities cannot be exported or imported arbitrarily. Commodities at one end of the scale will be exported and those at the other end imported, the dividing line being determined by demand conditions. Thus, for example, A and C cannot be exported and B imported.

The proof of this important result can be constructed as follows. Assuming only three commodities for convenience let the commodity price-ratio in country 1 be 10A = 10B = 10C. The factor cost of 10A, 10B and 10C must then all be the same. This is shown in Figure 14 by the isoquants for each of these amounts being tangential to the same factor outlay line *FF*. Suppose now that in country 2 commodity A is relatively cheaper than commodity B so that 10A is worth, say, 8B. The isoquants for 10A and 8B must then both be tangential to the same factor outlay line $F'F'$ in country 2. It is readily observed that the C isoquant that is tangential to $F'F'$ cannot be the one for eight units of C but for some amount less than that, say 5C. Hence if A is relatively cheaper than B in country 2, B must be relatively cheaper than C as was to be proved. It is clear that the result can be extended to a fourth or any number of additional commodities.

The reason for this result is not difficult to find. As Figure

14 shows if A is to be cheaper than B the factor price-ratio must shift in such a way that land is relatively cheaper than labour. But, since A is even more land-intensive in comparison with C than with B this means that A will be cheapened even more in terms of C. Hence B will be relatively cheaper than C. The country with a relative abundance of land will export goods from the land-intensive end of the spectrum of commodities and vice versa, demand conditions determining the point

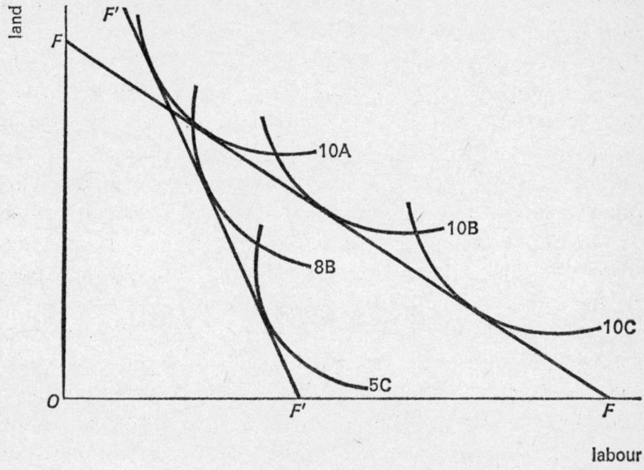

Figure 14

where the chain of comparative advantage is broken. Any commmodity exported by the land-abundant country will be more land-intensive than any commodity exported by the other country so that the Heckscher-Ohlin logic carries over to the multi-commodity case as well.[2]

The Ricardian case with fixed labour inputs is easily handled. Changing our notation briefly for convenience and letting

2. This result was proved mathematically in Jones (1956), but the geometric proof given here is simpler and more transparent.

a_i and b_i denote the fixed labour input in the ith commodity in countries A and B suppose that we have

$$\frac{a_1}{b_1} < \frac{a_2}{b_2} < \ldots < \frac{a_n}{b_n}, \qquad 1$$

that is to say country A is relatively most efficient in commodity 1, next most efficient in commodity 2 and so on down to commodity n in which she is relatively least efficient. If α and β are the money wage-rates (uniform for all sectors) in countries A and B, then whether commodity i is imported, exported or not traded by country A will depend on whether

$$a_i \alpha \gtreqless b_i \beta \qquad (i = 1, 2, \ldots, n) \qquad 2$$

i.e. on whether the money price is lower, higher or the same. The same condition can be written as

$$\frac{a_i}{b_i} \gtreqless \frac{\beta}{\alpha} \qquad 3$$

The money wage-rates can be taken as determined by the condition that the balance of payments must be in equilibrium. A country with a surplus will have an inflow of gold while the deficit country has an outflow. These gold flows will raise money wages in the surplus country and reduce them in the deficit country. Thus if A is in surplus, α will rise, with the result that fewer commodities will now be cheaper in A, so that some items will move the opposite way in international trade bringing about an equilibrium in the balance of payments. It will be observed that if commodity 7 is exported by A and commodity 8 by B then commodities 1 to 6 must be exported by A and commodities 9 to n by B as a result of condition **1**. Demand operating through the balance of payments mechanism and money wage-rates determines the point where the chain of comparative advantage is broken. This model, developed by such writers as Longfield, Mangoldt,

Edgeworth and Haberler forms the basis of a pioneering empirical study of the theory of comparative costs by Sir Donald MacDougall, which will be examined in chapter 5.

If the Ricardian model is expressed in terms of neutral differences in two-factor (or more) variable proportions production functions, then a_i and b_i need to be re-interpreted as scale factors measuring the efficiency of the factors in producing output and the inequality signs in **1** reversed to maintain the same order of comparative advantage. Demand will again break the chain but the mechanism by which it does so will no longer be simply through money wage-rates as before.

Throughout this chapter differences in factor endowment and in technology have been considered separately. If both are combined into a single model many interesting possibilities arise. In the two-country, multi-commodity case, for example, suppose that the ranking of goods in terms of land-intensity and in terms of relative technological superiority in the land-abundant country coincide. Then both the Heckscher-Ohlin *and* the Ricardian theorems will be valid since each country will export goods which use her abundant factor intensively as well as those goods in which her relative technological efficiency is highest. If, however, the two rankings are inversely correlated, so that the relative technological efficiency of the land-abundant country is lowest in the most land-intensive goods, then the two theories will conflict with each other and one of them will be true and the other false, depending upon whether factor endowments or technological differences exert the strongest influence. If the two rankings are not correlated at all then *neither* theory would have much validity since in each instance of trade in a commodity either factor endowment or technology could be the dominant influence so that there is no over-all pattern.

4 The Determinants of International Specialization II

In the last chapter a fairly exhaustive discussion of the two best known theories of international specialization was given. In the present chapter some interesting recent alternative approaches are examined. These are the 'vent for surplus', 'availability' and 'imitation gap' theories.

'Vent for Surplus'

The 'vent for surplus' approach originates in some remarks of Adam Smith in the *Wealth of Nations*, but although commented upon in J. H. Williams' well-known article of 1929 its modern revival is chiefly due to a recent attempt by Hla Myint to apply it to the analysis of the 'opening up' of traditional peasant economics in South-East Asia and Africa under colonial rule in the nineteenth century (Myint, 1958). The orthodox approach envisages an economy already on its production frontier before trade but then moving along this frontier in response to the opportunity to trade, expanding the production of the exported commodity and reducing that of the imported commodity. The same resources are used before and after, only a re-allocation between different uses taking place. In contrast to this the 'vent for surplus' approach postulates the existence of significant amounts of unused resources lying idle in the absence of the opportunity for international trade, which are drawn into export production once this opportunity arises, thus without causing any decline in other branches of local production. In this section we shall attempt to fit the Hla Myint argument into a simple model and subject it to a logical analysis, leaving open the question of whether or not it is a valid representation of the actual historical experience of the colonial economies.

Let the primitive traditional economy consist of two sectors, Handicrafts (H sector) and Food (F sector). The total number of man-hours available and the labour required per unit of each commodity define the line *XY*, in Figure 15, which is the boundary of the production possibilities set for the economy. The supply of land would impose a constraint on

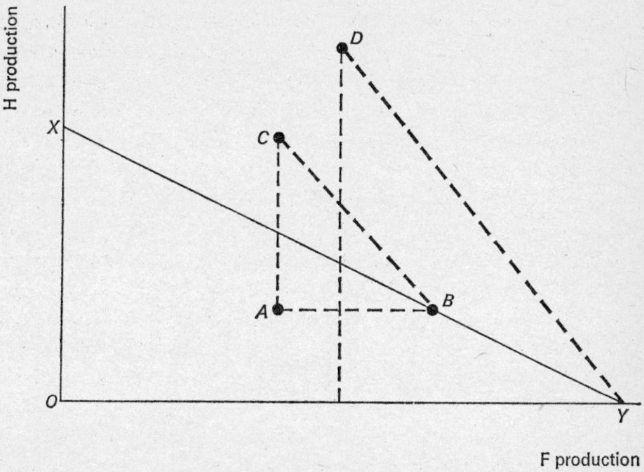

Figure 15

the level of production of the F sector, but it is assumed that initially this limit lies beyond the point *Y* in Figure 15 on the horizontal axis so that the supply of labour is what limits the production of both commodities. It is also assumed that whatever primitive tools are required are available to the labour force in the desired amount so that a separate capital constraint is not brought in.

The 'vent for surplus' model in the Hla Myint form does not only require surplus land but also surplus labour. Hence the economy must not be producing on the line *XY* but somewhere inside, as for instance at the point *A*. Exactly why this should be so, however, is not quite clear. The limitation on the F sector may be saturation of wants, that is, food is so plentiful that its marginal utility is zero for everybody as in some Polynesian island paradise. This explanation, however, immediately runs into some difficulties. If it is assumed that there is no specialization, and that members of the community can freely switch back and forth from the production of food and handicrafts, then what explains the limitation on the production of handicrafts? If the community is saturated with these as well, then the later response to the opportunity for trade has to be explained in terms of the import of entirely new goods that are not even imperfect substitutes for the traditional handicrafts. This could surely not have been the case. On the other hand if specialization is assumed, then there is the problem of how workers in the F sector obtain the products of the H sector, when the output of their own sector is so plentiful as to make it a free good.

An alternative explanation that seems more plausible can, however, be advanced in the following terms. The very low productivity of labour in the H sector, not only absolutely, but relative to the F sector with its abundance of fertile land, makes the terms of trade between food and handicrafts so unfavourable to the former that further production in the F sector for exchange with the H sector is not worth the effort. The *XY* curve is therefore not operative and the point A lies on a curve of the same slope as *XY* but to the left of it, the difference being due to the leisure enjoyed by workers in the F sector. The rate of exchange between the products of the two sectors is equal to the slope of the transformation curve passing through it which is the same as the slope of *XY*. Both aspects of Hla Myint's 'surplus productive capacity', land and labour, are now accounted for, of the former by its relative physical abundance and of the latter by the low opportunity cost of leisure.

The opening up of trade makes it possible for the economy to obtain a much higher exchange-ratio of manufactured goods (assumed to be the same articles as produced by the domestic H sector) in return for a unit of food. The effect of this is to raise the opportunity cost of leisure in terms of manufactures so that the full supply of labour from the F sector is provided now that it is so much more productive in terms of manufactures, the economy moving on to the *XY* transformation curve horizontally from *A* to *B*, the output of the F sector expanding while that of the H sector remains constant. Trade has thus provided a 'vent' for the surplus labour power and land of the traditional economy, rather than just an intersectoral shift of resources as in the orthodox comparative cost theory. The slope of the line *BC* measures the international terms of trade and *C* the new consumption point.

The next stage of the impact of trade on the peasant economy can be explained in more conventional terms. The handicraft sector obviously cannot compete with imported manufactures and so is wiped out, the labour being transferred into the F sector until the economy is completely specialized on food, *Y* being the production point and *D* the consumption point. The expansion of production and trade thus has a Smithian first phase and a Ricardian second phase (in the sense of the comparative cost theory being applicable to it).

Having reached *Y*, a new Smithian phase may be said to commence as population growth shifts the *XY* curve to the right, the surplus land making the extension of cultivation possible at constant or even decreasing cost. Production and export of food and import of manufactures all continue to grow. Finally however the point *Y′* in Figure 16 is reached where all the surplus land is exhausted. Further growth of population now requires production of manufactures locally if the increase in population is to be absorbed productively in the absence of any land-saving technical progress in the production of food. In terms of Figure 16 the economy has to climb from *Y′* to *Y″*.

During this phase trade will shrink as population growth will cut the exportable surplus of food with total production fixed. At unchanged terms of trade imports will also decline proportionately. If the additional population can be absorbed into a domestic manufacturing sector there will be an off-set to the decline in consumption of manufactures, although the cost of this domestic production will be higher than for imports. This does not imply by any means that local production of manufactures is in any sense 'uneconomic' or 'wasteful' from the point of view of comparative cost theory since, by assumption, the limited supply of land prevents any additional exports from being made. Of course it is possible to argue that efforts to increase the supply of land, or raise its yield per acre, would be more beneficial than to attempt industrialization, but the

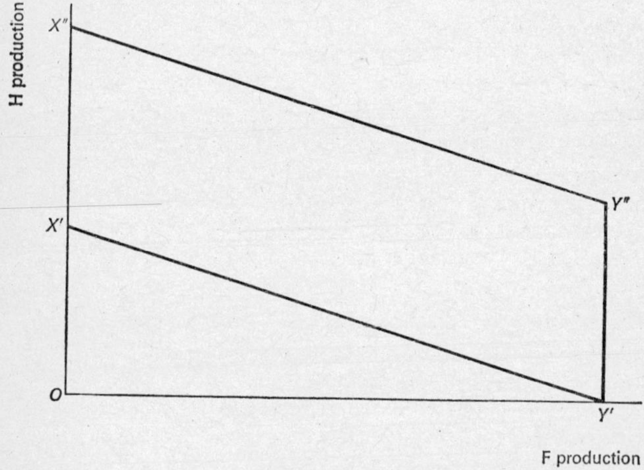

Figure 16

case for this cannot be made on the strength of the theory of comparative costs in its traditional form, which assumes fixed factor supplies and technical knowledge. Misunderstanding of this point has led to much criticism of attempts at industrialization in underdeveloped countries on the one hand, and to a violent rejection of the comparative cost theory as a reactionary doctrine for the perpetuation of the 'nineteenth century pattern' in the underdeveloped countries on the other. The above analysis indicates that there might not really be any logical contradiction between the two.

The question that now arises is whether this increase in

manufacturing production will take place without the need for any special intervention by the state. One difficulty is the shortage of capital for investment in factories using modern techniques of production. If insufficient investment is forthcoming the surplus labour may have to remain in the export sector for want of complementary facilities in the manufacturing sector to employ them. In terms of Figure 16 the point Y'' may lie outside a capital constraint line (not drawn). Hence measures by the state to raise capital formation by various devices open to it would be called for.

There is, however, another and more subtle difficulty that has been pointed out by W. A. Lewis (1954). This is the fact that workers in the export sector will obtain an income based on joint sharing of the product from the family plot assuming, as is valid in many cases, that this sector is based on peasant proprietorship. They will therefore only move to industry if they can get not only this income but a margin above it to cover their cost of movement. This wage, however, may be beyond the capacity of the nascent industrial sector to pay, even if sufficient capital formation for the setting up of factories and other facilities is available. A case for imposing a tariff on import of manufactures can therefore be made since this will raise the local price of these articles, enabling the local industry to be established. There will be a loss of welfare to consumers but the gain to the economy in terms of increased production might well be greater. A policy of taxing the export sector, preferably by a direct tax on land holdings, and using the proceeds to subsidize wages in the industrial sector is another way of achieving a similar result, perhaps at less social cost.

In the absence of the measures, trade might continue to contract because of increased consumption of a fixed food output by a larger population, without any expansion of domestic manufacturing production. Hla Myint asserts that this has actually been the case in the former colonial economies, and that this fact is consistent with the 'vent for surplus' theory, whereas it is inconsistent with the factor proportions theory which would predict a rise in the proportion of the labour-intensive commodity produced as the ratio of labour to land is increased. While it may be true that the Heckscher-Ohlin theory, assuming a smoothly operating price mechanism and technical flexibility, is not of much use in relation to the experience of the colonial export economies, it does not follow that the 'vent for surplus' theory is an adequate diagnosis of the phase where trade is contracting and domestic manufacturing production fails to substitute for it. The 'vent for surplus' doctrine is actually relevant only for the first phase, the movement from *A* to *B* in Figure 15. There is no reason why the failure to move from Y' to Y'' in Figure 16 should be connected to the fact that the opening up of trade took place from *A* rather than *B* in Figure 15. In the latter case there would be no Smithian first phase, the economy adjusting to the opportunity for trade in the conventional fashion by a re-allocation of resources, but there could still very well be the same Lewis-type situation at the end. Two essentially distinct arguments are used to explain a historical process, one for its beginning and one for the present situation, and 'vent for surplus' is an interesting tool for the analysis of the 'opening up' phase in the economic history of the former colonial territories but not for the contemporary problem. Indeed the 'vent for surplus' in the Lewis sense is in domestic manufacturing production and it is trade that prevents the opening from being taken.

'Availability'

Why does Kuwait export oil and South Africa export diamonds? To the 'man in the street' nothing could be more obvious. Is it not simply because Kuwait has oil-fields and South Africa has diamond mines? The availability of scarce natural resources such as these in only a few particular countries is put forward as a rival doctrine to the theory of comparative costs by I. B. Kravis, along with other sources of special national advantage such as the know-how for producing a complex new commodity, or the monopoly that Scotland enjoys for Scotch whisky and Switzerland for Swiss watches (Kravis, 1956).

In order to clarify the logic of the Kravis approach let us

consider the following highly unrealistic example. Suppose that there are *n* countries in the world and *n* commodities, and that each of the commodities requires an input that is not required by any of the others, and that each country has one and only one of these types of inputs. Suppose further that each country demands all *n* products, the proportions demanded of course depending upon the relative prices. Under these circumstances the supply of each commodity in the world market will be determined by the amount of the special input available in the country endowed with it, and the price determined by the total demand in all the countries. Assuming that each country finds its terms of trade sufficiently attractive to forgo some domestic consumption of the sole commodity it produces (in other words that its wants for foreign products are sufficiently urgent relative to its wants for the local product), a pattern of trade will emerge in which each country exports a single product and imports some or all of the others.

For such a world there would clearly be no reason to develop the theory of comparative advantage. The essence of this theory is the differences in the rates at which the trading countries can substitute the production of one good for another at the margin. If each country is physically able to produce only one commodity the subtleties of the theory of comparative advantage become irrelevant and the 'availability' theory would be all that is required. Even then, however, we must also introduce the taste factor as was done above to exclude the case of a country not participating in trade at all. With this qualification, availability of the special inputs is sufficient explanation of the pattern of exports.

Let us now take a big step towards the real world by allowing for the possibility that some countries are able to produce more than one good. For convenience suppose that there are four countries A, B, C and D and two goods, foodstuffs and manufactures, denoted F and M. Production of F requires agricultural land and production of M requires technological know-how; labour and capital are required by both commodities. We assume that countries A, B and C possess land and that countries B, C and D possess industrial know-how. Hence

A can only produce F and D only M, but B and C can produce both M and F. The marginal rate of transformation between M and F is taken as constant in both B and C, let us say 5F for 1M in B and 3F for 1M in C. All countries consume both M and F. Given the demand conditions and production possibilities an equilibrium price-ratio between M and F will be determined. A will always be an exporter of F, and D of M, but the trade pattern of B and C depends on the equilibrium price-ratio. Both would be exporters of F if the price-ratio is less than 3F for 1M and both would be exporters of M if it were greater than 5F for 1M. If the price-ratio were in between 5F for 1M and 3F for 1M, say 4F for 1M, then B would be an exporter of F and C an exporter of M.

We can now examine to what extent 'availability' serves to explain the pattern of trade in this model. Export of F from A to D and export of M from D to A can be explained purely in 'availability' terms since each country cannot produce the imported commodity at home. Trade between B and C, however, requires comparative cost theory to explain it since both countries can produce both goods. Trade between A and B and C or between D and B and C requires comparative cost for the B and C end and availability for the A or D end. Hence we see that the significance of the 'availability' theory for the actual pattern of world trade, as against that of the conventional comparative cost theory, varies inversely with the proportion of B to C and C to B type of trade to the total. So far as we know there is no empirical study of world trade along these lines and, although a host of conceptual and statistical difficulties can be imagined, it would be very worthwhile to have such a study, particularly if it could reveal trends over time. On the one hand, developing countries are producing a wider range of goods, but on the other hand, scientific and technical progress in the advanced countries is continuously introducing new commodities and it would therefore be interesting to see whether the 'gap' is widening or narrowing.

Our simple model demonstrates however that mere availability of a special input is not a sufficient explanation of why a country exports a particular commodity, since A, B and C all have land, but B and C might possibly be importers of F, and B, C and D all have industrial know-how, but B and C might be importers of M. The point is that the special inputs, even though they are specific to one good, will require complementary inputs of a more flexible type which have other uses and so the relative efficiency of these resources in producing the good in question and other alternatives must be considered, as in the theory of comparative costs.

We shall now try to relate the 'availability' approach to the factor proportions one. In the above example let B and C both have the identical endowment of labour and capital and the same technical knowledge for producing M and F but let B have more land than C. Both countries would then be able to produce the same amount of M if all resources were devoted to this purpose, but B could produce more F for any given volume of M less than the maximum since she has more land. The production-possibilities curves would be as shown in Figure 17 with that of B lying outside. At terms of trade represented by the slope of *PP* and *P'P'* and demand proportions represented by the slope of the line from the origin it can be seen that B will export F. It is the higher ratio of land to capital and labour in B that explains why that country exports F rather than C. Factor proportions have therefore to be brought in, after all.

On the other hand it is also possible to construct cases in which the 'availability' approach comes off better than the factor proportions one. For instance suppose that M always has a higher capital-labour ratio than F and that B has a higher aggregate capital-labour ratio than C, the same technological knowledge being available in both countries. Production of F requires land and of M iron-ore deposits, the former being available only in B and the latter only in C. Then B will be an exporter of F, and C of M; in other words the capital-abundant country will export the labour-intensive good and vice versa. The factor proportions argument applied in this way would give the wrong answer, whereas taking note of the availability of land in B and of iron-ore deposits in C would give the right one. Of course it is true that the factor proportions approach could be used in such a way as to embrace natural resources as well, so that we could say that B is land-abundant and therefore exports the land-intensive commodity, whereas C is abundantly endowed with iron-ore deposits and hence exports the 'iron-intensive' commodity. But since the list of specific types of natural resources is a very long one, generalizing the factor

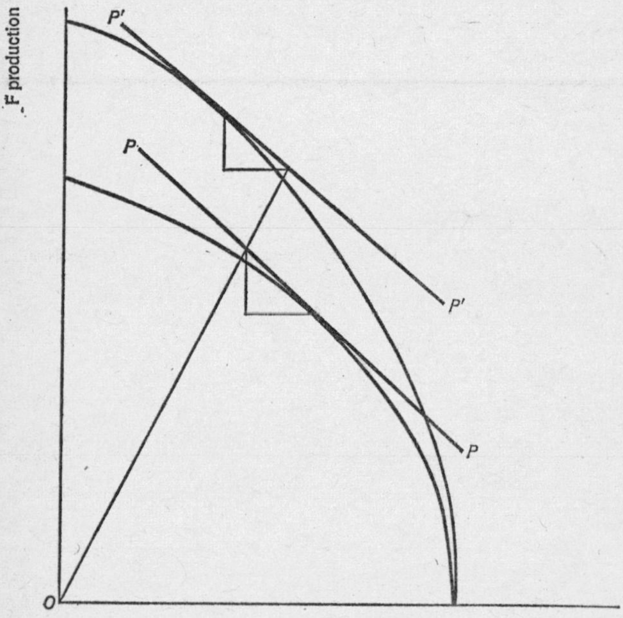

Figure 17

proportions approach in this way makes it a very clumsy tool. Even with only three factors we cannot say whether the more capital-abundant or the more land-abundant country is more likely to export a commodity that requires both capital and land relatively more intensively than labour.

The Scotch whisky and Swiss watch type of 'availability' argument requires separate consideration. Here what is emphasized is the fact that foreign consumers have an 'irrational' attachment to the source of a particular product because of past excellence or advertising or some other reason. They are willing to pay more for the commodity from the country in question than for an objectively identical article from another country. Hence a country that is able to produce a commodity of this type will enjoy more favourable terms of trade if it exports this commodity than if foreign consumers did not have this preference. Can we, however, say that this preference of foreign consumers is either a necessary or sufficient condition or both for the country to export the commodity? Clearly it is not necessary, since it could very well be that even without the special attachment of foreign consumers the country would still be an exporter, although of a smaller volume. It is also not sufficient since in spite of the extra price that can be obtained for the commodity in question it may be more profitable to use the required resources for the production and export of a commodity for which the country enjoys no special reputation. However what Kravis is driving at is that in actual fact without this preference there would be no trade in such items since cost differences are too small between nations for commodities in which technical knowledge is broadly the same and the resources required are commonly available. This again is an empirical question on which we do not have sufficient knowledge.

New Commodities and the 'Imitation Gap'

Yet another aspect of the 'availability' theory is the emergence of new products as the result of scientific research such as synthetic materials, transistors and computers. For a time the innovating country enjoys a monopoly and others have to import it until such time as they can learn to produce it themselves. Trade is thus created for the duration of the 'imitation gap'. Since the continuous progress of modern science is continually creating new products this aspect of world trade is not only permanent, but growing fast in relative importance to trade in more traditional types of manufactures, although the commodities that have yet to be imitated are changing over time. This theory might well be called Schumpeterian since it is an application of his concepts of innovation and imitation to international trade.

Kravis' original suggestion was more fully analysed in a stimulating article by M. V. Posner (1961). C. P. Kindleberger also has a very interesting chapter on this subject in his *Foreign Trade and the National Economy* (1962). The imitation lag is broken up by Posner into three components – the 'foreign reaction lag' which is the time taken for the first foreign firm to begin the attempt to produce the new commodity, the 'domestic reaction lag' which is the time required for other domestic producers to follow suit, and the learning period which is the time taken for the domestic industry to master the technique of producing the new commodity and selling it in the home market. Trade in the new commodity, however, will not take place for the full duration of the imitation lag since consumers will also take some time to acquire the taste for it. This 'demand lag' must therefore be subtracted from the 'imitation lag' to obtain the period during which imports of the new commodity will take place. A quick response by local producers and a slow response by local consumers will therefore reduce the period for which trade in the new commodity takes place. On the other hand, it could be argued that it is local consumer response to the foreign product which causes local producers to imitate, so that the two lags are not independent of each other.

Posner defines the 'dynamism' of a country in international trade as a function of the rate at which it innovates, that is the number of new commodities it introduces per unit of time, and the speed with which it imitates foreign innovations. If one of two trading partners has a higher degree of dynamism, for either or both reasons, than the other, then the deficit on trade in the new commodities can only be made up by the more sluggish partner by export of traditional commodities at less favourable prices. This additional trade in old commodities is thus induced by the entry of the new commodities so that some traditional trade even is caused by the dynamic factors of innovation and imitation. This type of trade between 'unequal partners' has been vividly analysed by Thomas Balogh (1963) who points out that free trade between them leads to the weaker partner becoming a 'hewer of wood and drawer of water'. The weaker partner gets caught in a vicious circle with her original lack of dynamism causing balance of payments problems which, in turn, prevent her from investing on a large scale in modernization of plant and equipment which alone can raise her degree of dynamism. The post-war British economy is of course the classic case of this situation. On the other hand where the degree of dynamism is relatively similar, and/or where there exist flexible systems of international monetary settlement, trade can stimulate a process of all-round development as innovations from each country are quickly imitated in the others. The remarkable expansion of trade and growth in the European common market countries can perhaps be explained in this way even though many of the new commodities introduced might have been imitations of earlier American innovations. Recently, however, the French in particular have had a striking record of independent innovations.

One important question is the persistence of the comparative advantage in the new commodity of the innovating country. Although imitation follows in some countries, the innovator will have an advantage in third markets as a result of its earlier start and hence greater experience with the production of the commodity. This sort of 'learning by doing' effect is now being widely analysed in different fields of economic theory and it seems that international trade will be one in which it can be applied very fruitfully. Posner has the credit for introducing the concept into recent trade theory, but it should be remembered that this effect is the essence of List's case for protection way back in the middle of the nineteenth century.

On the other hand the imitating country may be better endowed with some input that is important for the production of the new commodity than the innovating country. Kindleberger cites the case of Japanese export of transistors, an American innovation, to the U.S.A. after a short lag, the relative abundance of skilled labour in Japan being the cause. This suggests that once the technology for the new commodity is diffused factor proportions may take over again as the cause of trade. There is also a considerable literature, going back at least to Thorstein Veblen, on the 'penalty of taking the lead'. The classic illustration of this is the British railways in which the narrow gauge and small goods wagons that were adapted to conditions at the time, when Britain was the first country to introduce railways, later proved to be a drag on progress as expansion took place. Imitators like Germany and the U.S.A. were able to adapt their railways more successfully to later conditions and this may have been an important factor in enabling them to wrest industrial supremacy from Britain.

These opposing tendencies make it dangerous to regard the advantage of the innovator to be cumulative. Balogh's 'unequal partners' approach, for example, led him to expect the post-war dollar shortage to be more chronic than it was, and also to predict that Germany would dominate the common market to the detriment of France and Italy.

It is also interesting to attempt to relate the innovation theory itself to the factor proportions approach. Posner points out rightly that they are logically independent since two countries with exactly the same factor endowment will generally innovate in different particular lines, there being something of a random character to the whole process. However, it also seems true to say that the capacity to undertake 'research and development' in a deliberate, systematic way, which is the source of most modern innovations, is itself dependent on a relatively large endowment of capital. Within a group of capital-abundant countries the generation of different particular innovations in each country will largely depend on accidental factors so that these are a separate cause of trade. But if we look at world trade as a whole we would find new products being exported only by countries with a high proportion of capital to other factors, which they can profitably invest in setting up research laboratories, maintaining teams of scientists and experimenting with different uses and production processes for the new goods that have been invented. Even within the capital-abundant group different degrees of what Posner calls 'dynamism' may be systematically related to differences in the relative availability of capital. For example, the persistent 'technological gap' which is supposed to exist between U.S.A. and Western Europe may be determined largely by the greater availability of capital in the U.S.A. Other ways of looking at the problem from the factor proportions point of view would be to say that the supply of 'risk-taking' (an essential factor with new commodities), or the supply of scientists and research workers, is relatively large in the innovating countries. Greater availability of capital however is precisely what may permit greater risk-taking and scientific education.

The connexion between factor proportions and new commodities operates from the demand side as well. Scarcity of labour in relation to capital prompts the search for labour-saving devices and thus generates a stream of new products such as various types of automatic machinery and household appliances. High capital-labour ratios imply high *per capita* incomes and thus create the market for new consumer goods. It can be argued that although the demand for new commodities may be greatest in capital-abundant countries with higher *per capita* incomes it does not necessarily follow that these countries must supply their own wants in this direction. May not other countries innovate in the new lines to supply the market in the most capital-rich country, if their resources and factor endowments are better suited to the production of these items? The answer is that innovation requires detailed knowledge of potential markets and also a sufficient degree of certainty of access to these markets. These factors mean that domestic producers will always have an advantage on new commodities for their own market since they are in the closest contact with it, and also do not have to worry about tariffs and other trade barriers cutting them off after substantial investment is made in research and development.

Once the new commodities have appeared in the country with the highest *per capita* income and endowment of capital per worker they can find markets in countries where the degree of labour scarcity and the demand pattern is closest to conditions prevailing in the innovating country. The Swedish economist Linder (1961) has emphasized the importance of similarity in demand patterns as a cause of trade.

Increasing returns to scale in the production of the new commodity will give an added advantage to the innovating country. It takes time and large investments of resources to get production levels to the optimum scale, and it is a familiar proposition in the theory of oligopoly that substantial increasing returns can act as an effective 'barrier to entry'. Applied to international trade this can provide a further explanation of patterns of comparative advantage for new commodities.

5 Empirical Testing of Theories of International Specialization

In the last two chapters we have outlined the logical structure of the various theories of international specialization. It now remains to examine these theories in the light of empirical evidence for and against them. In spite of the sophistication of the logic, the scientific immaturity of the subject is reflected by the fact that although the theoretical developments that we have been discussing have taken place over the period of a century and a half, empirical testing of the theories, as opposed to mere descriptive studies of trade patterns, began only in about 1950. The 'pure' theory of international trade has lagged behind the 'monetary' theory in this respect, since empirical tests of the classical theory of the transfer mechanism were conducted by Viner and Williams as far back as the 1920s. In spite of the late start, however, very rapid progress is now being made and the cumulative process of interaction between the formulation of theories and the testing of these against empirical data that is the hallmark of true science can now be seen to be taking place.

In discussing the results so far obtained in the empirical testing of the theories of comparative advantage, we will avoid consideration of detailed questions such as the accuracy of the data used in the tests and the adequacy, or otherwise, of the particular statistical techniques employed by the researchers. The focus will be on broader methodological aspects such as whether the tests do really confirm or refute hypotheses which are logical implications of the theoretical structures. This is particularly important in fields such as the present one, where the theory is cast in a very abstract form with the result that the connexion between the variables emphasized in the theory and measurable magnitudes in the real world is somewhat tenuous.

Labour Productivity and Classical Comparative Costs

The pioneering attempt at empirical testing of a theory of international specialization was made by Sir Donald MacDougall (1951, 1952). Studies on the comparative productivity of labour in manufacturing industries in Britain and the U.S.A. turned up sufficient data to enable him to devise an ingenious test of the Ricardian theory of the pattern of trade, in which it is predicted that the country with the lower comparative *labour* costs for any commodity will be the exporter of that commodity. In the case of Britain and the U.S.A., however, the bilateral trade between them is only a small fraction of the total trade of each. What MacDougall tested, therefore, was the extent to which the *relative* exports of each country to third markets in the rest of the world was connected with its comparative labour cost position *vis à vis* the other.

Wage-rates in the manufacturing sector were roughly twice as high in the U.S.A. as in Britain. MacDougall therefore argued that the U.S.A. should be the dominant exporter to third markets of products in which her labour productivity was more than twice as high as in Britain, and that similarly Britain should be the dominant exporter wherever her labour productivity was less than twice as high. Where labour productivity in the U.S.A. was roughly twice as high MacDougall expected to observe equal shares for each country in exports to third markets.

For the twenty-five products for which he had data MacDougall obtained what appear to be very good results. The ratio of U.S. to British exports in third markets was in most cases higher whenever her ratio of labour productivity was higher, the coefficient of correlation being 0·8. The dividing line between British and American dominance in third markets, however, was not where U.S. productivity was twice as high but where it was two and a half times as high. MacDougall put forward imperial preference, the tariff advantage enjoyed by

British goods in the countries linked to her politically, as a major possible explanation of this phenomenon.

While MacDougall's statistical analysis has not so far been seriously questioned there has been considerable comment and criticism of the theoretical interpretation and significance of his results. J. Bhagwati (1964), in his authoritative survey of the pure theory of international trade, has gone so far as to say that MacDougall's study has little to do with the question of an empirical test of the Ricardian theory of comparative cost. He argues that there are two steps to the hypothesis that MacDougall is testing:

1. That relative labour costs are correlated with relative prices.

2. That relative export shares of two countries in third markets are correlated with relative prices of their exports.

He asserts that it is only the first step in the argument that is derived from the Ricardian theory while differences in preferences, quality, distance, historical links and so on make it unlikely that Ricardo or anyone else would ever have expected the second relationship to hold. The fact that MacDougall has found strong evidence in favour of the hypothesis thus comes as a surprise since according to him there is no theoretical basis for predicting it. The downward sloping demand curve that theory postulates as facing any *one* trading country for its exports lends no justification to a cross-section study of two different countries, where the varying position of the separate demand curves facing the two countries can swamp the effects of differences in prices between them. To test 1 he uses the data provided by MacDougall and later investigators and he finds no significant correlation between relative labour costs and relative export prices. He therefore concludes that instead of the data verifying the Ricardian theory they actually refute it.

It is difficult to agree with Bhagwati in holding that proposition 2 is irrelevant to the Ricardian theory. In its most rigid form the Ricardian theory would predict that the country with the lower labour costs for any product would be the *sole* exporter to the third markets of that product, since markets are assumed to be perfect and transport costs zero. On this rigid interpretation the test that MacDougall conducted would refute the theory; it would not, however, be irrelevant to the theory. No one would really expect, though, that the theory would have any chance of being confirmed if it is put in such extreme form. Differences in quality, transport costs, tariff policies in the third markets towards imports from the two rivals and so on would prevent the cheaper producer from capturing the entire market. However, the hypothesis could be made that the combined difference that all these compensating factors make in one direction or the other is uniform for all products, so that a country's relative share of the third market would rise with the relative cheapness of its exports. This would seem to be a perfectly permissible modification of the rigid version of the Ricardian theory and MacDougall has shown that the hypothesis is in conformity with the facts that he has been able to obtain.

MacDougall found that when costs were the same in the two countries American exports were only about two-fifths of British. This can be taken as evidence of the general advantage that British exports enjoyed due to such factors as her commercial reputation due to her being the pioneer industrial nation, her more extensive international financial network, her influence on overseas territories, imperial preference and so on. As the productivity differential increased further, however, the U.S. share rose until, as mentioned earlier, equality was attained when her productivity was about two and a half times the British and was greater than the British share when the differential exceeded this.

It thus appears that MacDougall's study is relevant to the question of testing the Ricardian theory empirically and does in fact provide evidence in favour of it. It could well be that factors other than labour costs, such as capital costs for example, move in the opposite direction to differences in labour costs so that no systematic pattern linking productivity with export shares could be observed. MacDougall's study has ruled out this possibility for the cases that he observed.

What remains a problem, however, is the fact that, using the same data as MacDougall, Bhagwati was not able to find a significant correlation between relative labour costs and relative export prices. MacDougall obtained high correlations between relative labour costs and relative export shares and also between relative export prices and relative export shares. This leads us to expect that relative labour costs would be highly correlated with relative export prices but Bhagwati has shown that it is not so. A genuine statistical puzzle thus appears to have been turned up, to await solution by further research.

For the moment two possibilities are open. One may choose to accept the Bhagwati result that relative labour costs are not correlated with relative export prices, and take this as evidence refuting the Ricardian theory, since it is only through relative export prices that relative labour costs can influence relative export shares. This would mean treating the high correlation that MacDougall obtained between relative labour costs and relative export shares as a statistical phenomenon for which no satisfactory theoretical explanation can be found. On the other hand, one may accept the MacDougall results and treat the Bhagwati correlations as requiring further refinement and analysis before they are accepted.

Our discussion has thus shown that it is not always (if ever!) that a single set of observations can either confirm or refute a theoretical hypothesis in a clear-cut decisive fashion.

MacDougall's lead has been followed more recently by Stern (1962) and Balassa (1963), using more extensive data for later periods. On the whole the results obtained by them are in conformity with those of MacDougall. Stern repeats MacDougall's procedure but with data for 1950 instead of 1937, when the average wage in the U.S. had risen to about three and a half times the British. Stern found that when labour costs were equalized U.S. exports were still less than the British, as in MacDougall's study, but that they had risen from about two-fifths to about four-fifths. This result is significant in relation to the hypothesis that the MacDougall finding was due to the general advantage that British goods enjoyed in 1937 due to Britain's early industrial, commercial and financial leadership and to her political influence. By 1950 this advantage was very much reduced so we would expect the relative American export performance to improve and Stern's calculations show that in fact it did do so quite significantly. Bhagwati's correlations between relative labour costs and relative export prices, however, show equally poor results with the Stern and Balassa data as with MacDougall's original figures.

The Heckscher-Ohlin Theory and the Leontief Paradox

Soon after MacDougall's pioneering test of the classical comparative cost doctrine Professor W. Leontief (1953) of Harvard published what has now become a famous article testing the Heckscher-Ohlin factor endowment theory of international specialization. It was the first application to international trade theory of the powerful new technique of input-output analysis, developed by Professor Leontief himself. As such it has had a host of imitators and the list is bound to grow as detailed input-output tables for more countries become available. More important than the use of a powerful novel approach, however, was the result of the Leontief test. He found, to his own and everybody else's surprise, that in 1947 the U.S.A. apparently exported *labour-intensive* products and imported *capital-intensive* ones. Since everyone believes that the U.S.A. is the country whose labour force is by far the most richly endowed with capital in the world, the test was apparently an outright refutation of the Heckscher-Ohlin theory, the *a priori* plausibility of which was accepted by most economists, so that the result was soon termed the Leontief Paradox. A flood of articles and even books has appeared, attempting to 'explain' or 'dispel' the Paradox, and contributing greatly to our theoretical and factual knowledge of international trade in the process. One is almost tempted to wish for another paradox to be uncovered, so fruitful has been the effect of this first one.

The nature of Leontief's test must first be explained. The question that he posed was what would be the effect on the use of capital and labour in the U.S.A. if total exports and imports were each to be reduced by a million dollars, and the previously imported goods replaced by similar commodities produced domestically. The test therefore excluded such imports as Guatemalan bananas or Brazilian coffee, for which no import-competing industry exists in the U.S.A. The distribution of the million dollars worth of exports and imports over specific commodity sectors was made proportionally to the importance of these sectors in total exports and imports. Leontief then used his techniques of input-output analysis to estimate the amount of production from each sector of the economy that would be required, directly and indirectly, for the million dollars worth of exports and imports distributed in this manner. The next step was to calculate the capital and labour inputs needed for these levels of production in each sector. The sectoral estimates were then added to give figures for the total capital and labour required, directly and indirectly, for a million dollars worth of exports and import replacements respectively. The final result of the calculations is shown in the table below.

	Exports	*Import replacement*
Capital (in dollars)	2,550,780	3,091,339
Labour (in man-years)	182,313	170,004
Capital-labour ratio (dollars per man-year)	14,010	18,180

It can be seen that exports embody slightly more labour and considerably less capital than import replacements of the same value, and this is what constitutes the Paradox.

Criticisms and explanations were not slow in coming. Swerling observed that 1947, the year that Leontief selected for the test because comprehensive input-output data were available for it, was a highly abnormal one as far as trade flows were concerned (Swerling, 1954). He also pointed out possible biases in the way in which the aggregation of commodities into sectors was carried out. Leontief attempted to deal with these and other statistical problems in a later article and it now appears to be fairly certain that, imperfect though the data are, the Paradox cannot be dispelled on this ground (Leontief, 1956).

The main explanations of the Leontief Paradox that have been offered are listed below:

(a) U.S. labour is much superior to foreign labour so that the American capital stock is relatively less abundant than abroad when U.S. labour is converted into the equivalent foreign labour.

(b) U.S. demand patterns are biased towards capital-intensive goods so that in the absence of trade these goods would be relatively more expensive there in spite of the greater relative abundance of capital, so that the U.S. becomes an importer of these goods and an exporter of labour-intensive goods.

(c) U.S. imports are actually more labour-intensive than her exports and it is only the U.S. import competing industries that are more capital-intensive than U.S. exports.

(d) Trade patterns also depend upon natural resource endowments, which are scarce in the U.S. relatively to *both* labour and capital, making the U.S. an importer of natural resource-intensive commodities. If domestic production has to substitute for these imports relatively more capital than labour may be required as compared with exports, but the reason for this is simply that the U.S. has to make good her deficiency of natural resources by using capital which is relatively more abundant than labour.

(e) U.S. exports have a higher ratio of skilled to unskilled labour than her import replacement industries, and the greater education and training embodied in the labour force of the export industries represents additional 'human capital' required for these industries. When human capital requirements are added to physical capital requirements it may turn out that exports are more capital-intensive.

Before going on to discuss each of these explanations in detail it should be noticed that they have different implications for the validity of the Heckscher-Ohlin theory. The first explanation would reconcile the Paradox with the Heckscher-Ohlin theory since the U.S. could become labour-abundant relative to the rest of the world if the efficiency differential between U.S. and foreign labour is sufficiently large. The second and third explanations would, however, result in the refutation of the Heckscher-Ohlin theory since the second implies that the capital- (labour-) abundant country does not export the capital- (labour-) intensive good and the reversal of relative factor intensities that the third explanation relies on must result in one of the two trading areas contradicting the Heckscher-Ohlin theory. To see this suppose that commodity A is exported by the U.S. and commodity B imported by it. The explanation says that B is labour-intensive in the rest of the world, which is labour-abundant, and this squares with the theory, but B is relatively capital-intensive in the U.S. and so the capital-abundant U.S. exports its labour-intensive good A, which is contrary to the theory. On the other hand if the U.S. exported B the labour-abundant rest of the world must export A, which is relatively capital-intensive there. Either way the theory would be refuted. The last two explanations can be made consistent with the Heckscher-Ohlin theory, but this requires extension of the simple two-factor model that has been mainly used so far to take into account different grades of labour and natural resources. In his original presentation Ohlin did allow for a multiplicity of factors but only in a very loose general way. For the theory to be capable of yielding specific empirically refutable predictions it must be formulated in an explicit analytical fashion.

The explanations of the Leontief Paradox will now be examined in turn.

Superiority of U.S. labour

This explanation was put forward by Leontief himself as the most plausible reconciliation of his results with the Heckscher-Ohlin theory. He quite arbitrarily gave a figure of one average man-year in the U.S. being equal to *three* man-years abroad, thus cutting the relative capital endowment per unit of labour in the U.S. to one-third of its conventional value. It should be realized that Leontief is saying much more than that labour productivity in the U.S. is three times as high as the average in the rest of the world. Productivity figures reflect capital endowment per worker which is higher in the U.S. What he is asserting is that U.S. labour is three times more productive than foreign labour *with the same amount of capital per head.* He attributes this difference mainly to the superior organization of American industries. This raises the question, however, of why it is only labour and not capital as well that superior organization in the U.S. can render more productive. An important study on international comparison of production functions in various industries by Arrow, Chenery, Minhas and Solow indicated that efficiency differences did exist between countries but that these tended to be neutral as between capital and labour (Arrow *et al.*, 1961). If superior U.S. organization makes both capital and labour more efficient than abroad in the same proportion, then the capital-labour ratio in the U.S. will be the same as before and the Paradox cannot be explained by converting the U.S. into a labour-abundant country. In the face of the contrary evidence cited and the absence of any empirical evidence in support of the hypothesis it must be rejected.

Demand pattern

The possibility that the Leontief Paradox might be due to the U.S. demand pattern being biased towards capital-intensive goods can be found in the work of several authors such as S. Valvanis-Vail (1954), R. Robinson (1956) and R. Jones (1956). As was shown in chapter 3 the assumption of identical tastes in the trading areas can still be consistent with the existence of such a bias because *per capita* income levels may differ, thus leading to different proportions of the commodities being demanded at the same price-ratio unless income-elasticities of demand are unity. If capital-intensive goods have income-elasticity greater than unity and labour-intensive goods less than unity, it may be that the capital-abundant and therefore higher *per capita* income country will have a higher relative price of capital-intensive goods in the absence of trade, the demand bias in favour of these goods more than off-setting the supply bias in the opposite direction. The situation may be described by saying that the *physically* abundant factor is economically scarce and vice versa.

The point can be clarified by an example. Supposing that

automobiles are capital-intensive and wheat is labour-intensive. A rich capital-abundant country may have such a strong demand for automobiles that these would be relatively scarce in this country in the absence of trade, whereas in a poorer, labour-abundant country the weaker demand may make them cheaper. Hence automobiles may be exported by the labour-abundant country and wheat, the demand for which will be a smaller fraction of total income in the richer country, imported by the labour-abundant country.

This explanation may have a certain intuitive plausibility but so far no solid empirical evidence has been advanced either in favour of or against it. A study by Houthakker indicates that demand patterns show considerable similarly between nations but, as has been pointed out, this can still be consistent with a biased demand pattern in one direction or the other due to income-elasticities differing from unity, as they certainly do (Houthakker, 1957). What would be required to test truly this explanation is a study linking empirical estimates of income-consumption coefficient and capital-labour ratios of specific commodities or commodity groups. Houthakker has pioneered work in one direction and the previously cited work of Arrow, Chenery, Minhas and Solow in the other, so perhaps it will not be too long before an integrated study is made.

Factor-intensity reversals

One of the earliest comments on the Leontief Paradox, containing most of the explanations that have been put forward, was by P. T. Ellsworth (1954). His main point, however, appears to have been that all that the Heckscher-Ohlin theory says is that the capital-labour ratio of exports from a capital-abundant country should be higher than the capital-labour ratio of its imports from labour-abundant countries in their own production of these goods. Hence only half of Leontief's calculations, those dealing with the capital-labour ratio of U.S. exports, was relevant. For imports from each country of origin he should have computed the capital-labour ratio on the basis of input-output studies *of those economies* and aggregated the result with weights proportional to the volume of imports from each country. If the capital-labour ratio of imports computed in this way was higher than that of U.S. exports a genuine paradox would have been created. However, since Leontief had no input-output studies of foreign countries to rely on, he was unable to make the correct comparison and instead fell back on the capital-labour ratio of import substitution in the United States which, in Ellsworth's view, was irrelevant. Furthermore the facts that the capital-labour ratio of U.S. import substitution was higher than of U.S. exports merely showed that if a capital-abundant country has to replace labour-intensive imports by inefficient domestic production it minimizes the inefficiency by using capital-intensive methods, suited to its relatively abundant factor.

Although there seems to be some robust common sense to this point of view closer examination reveals that it is an untenable interpretation of the Heckscher-Ohlin theory. What Ellsworth is saying is that the more capital- (labour-) abundant a country is the more capital- (labour-) intensive will be the *methods* by which its exports are produced. This is a plausible and interesting hypothesis in its own right but it is *not* the Heckscher-Ohlin proposition. The essence of that proposition is the attempt to link factor endowments to trade patterns by postulating the possibility of a ranking of goods by capital-intensity, and predicting that capital-abundant countries will export goods from the upper end of the scale and labour-abundant ones from the lower. Ellsworth's interpretation leaves the type of commodities exported by each country completely open and is therefore not a theory of comparative advantage at all.

On Ellsworth's interpretation the same goods are capital-intensive in the U.S. but labour-intensive abroad. This can arise as a result of differences in production functions or as a result of the 'strong' factor-intensity hypothesis for identical production functions (mentioned in chapter 3) not holding. In this situation, as pointed out earlier, one of the countries must violate the proposition that the capital- (labour-) abundant country exports the capital- (labour-) intensive good.

The question that now arises is the empirical one of whether factor-intensities do tend to reverse themselves or not as between countries. Samuelson expressed the view that, if production functions were similar in the different countries, it would be highly unlikely that the 'strong' factor-intensity hypothesis would fail to hold (Samuelson, 1951–2). This judgement was not contradicted on either empirical or purely speculative grounds until the work of B. S. Minhas (1963) appeared.

The origin of Minhas' demonstration of the strong possibility and empirical existence of reversibility was the work he did in conjunction with Arrow, Chenery and Solow cited earlier, on a cross-country comparative study of production functions for several industries. In this study they introduced a particular type of production function, the Constant Elasticity of Substitution or CES production function, and found that it fitted the data that they gathered quite well, industry by industry. What Minhas showed in his later individual application to international trade was that so long as the elasticity of substitution (a measure of the extent to which capital and labour are substitutable for each other in the production of a given type of output) is constant in all industries but differs between industries, which is *a priori* highly likely, reversibility must occur and in fact did occur in some factual cases that he presented.

In view of the evident importance of this contention the derivation of the result is given below. The CES production function may be written as:

$$V = (AK^{-\beta} + \alpha L^{-\beta})^{-1/\beta},$$

where V is output, K capital, L labour and A, a and β are parameters, the value of which depends on the characteristics of production for each type of output. The marginal productivities of capital and labour can be obtained by partial differentiation with respect to K and L so that we have:

$$\frac{\partial V}{\partial L} = \alpha \left(\frac{V}{L}\right)^{\beta+1},$$

$$\frac{\partial V}{\partial K} = A \left(\frac{V}{K}\right)^{\beta+1}.$$

The marginal rate of substitution between capital and labour, denoted by x is:

$$x = \frac{\partial V}{\partial L} \bigg/ \frac{\partial V}{\partial K} = \frac{\alpha}{A}\left(\frac{K}{L}\right)^{\beta+1}.$$

Taking logarithms of both sides we have:

$$\log x = \log\left(\frac{\alpha}{A}\right) + (\beta+1)\log\left(\frac{K}{L}\right).$$

Now the elasticity of substitution, σ, is defined as the proportionate change in the capital-labour ratio divided by the proportionate change in the factor price-ratio which, under perfect competition, is equal to the marginal rate of substitution between capital and labour. We therefore have:

$$\sigma = \frac{d\log(K/L)}{d\log x} = \frac{1}{(\beta+1)}.$$

The logarithmic form of the equation for x, and therefore for the factor price-ratio (w/r) where w and r are the prices of labour and capital, can therefore be plotted as straight lines, as shown in Figure 18 below for two industries, 1 and 2.

If σ is the same for industries 1 and 2 then β must be the same and the curves would be parallel to each other. Hence, whatever the factor price-ratio one industry will always be more capital-intensive or labour-intensive than the other. However, if σ differs between industries then the slopes will differ so that the curves must intersect at some point, as in Figure 18. To the left of the intersection point commodity 2 is more capital-intensive but to the right of it commodity 1 is. Hence the intersection point is a 'cross-over' point, at which a reversal of factor-intensities takes place. Postulate that production functions are identical for the same industry in different countries, let commodity 1 be what is imported by the U.S. and 2 what is exported by it, and suppose that the factor price-ratio in the U.S. is to the right of the cross-over point while abroad it is to the left. This will neatly explain the Leontief Paradox.

It is clearly impossible that all industries will have exactly the same elasticity of substitution. However, the 'cross-over' points must occur at factor price-ratios that are within the empirically relevant range, spanned say by India at one extreme and the U.S. at the other. Using data for twenty-four industries and nineteen countries in a cross-section analysis Minhas turned up five instances of factor-intensity reversals in the relevant range. The industries concerned were textiles, non-ferrous metals, dairy products, pulp and paper, basic chemicals and grain mill products.

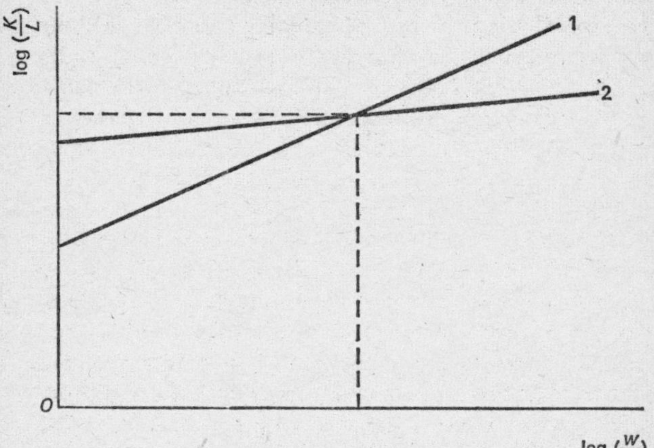

Figure 18

In addition to this direct demonstration on the basis of the estimated values of the parameters of the CES production functions for these industries Minhas tried to show the existence of reversibility by an indirect test. He argued that if the strong factor-intensity hypothesis is valid and production functions are identical then, if we take countries with widely disparate factor price-ratios such as Japan and the U.S.A., the ranking of industries by capital-intensity in the two countries must be similar. In a test involving twenty industries he found that the correlation between the U.S. ranking and the Japanese ranking was poor, thus indicating the likelihood of reversibility.

It did not take long for both Minhas' tests to come under fire.

Using Minhas' own data Leontief showed that out of 210 possible reversals he was only able to obtain seventeen and in most of these cases the curves were so close together as to be virtually from the same production function (Leontief, 1964). The evidence, he felt, is more in favour of the 'strong' factor-intensity hypothesis than against it. The ranking test was attacked by Ball on the ground that the list included agriculture and many industries based on natural resources (Ball, 1966). In these cases, he argued, the assumption of identical production functions is a very unrealistic one. Once these industries were removed the rank correlations increased significantly. Moroney conducted a similar test for several regions in the U.S.A. and found that the result supported the 'strong' factor intensity hypothesis (Moroney, 1967). Hence, at least as of the present moment, it appears that reversibility of factor-intensities cannot be accepted as a major explanation of the Leontief Paradox.

Natural resources

Economists have traditionally classified land, labour and capital as the 'factors of production'. The limitation to only the latter two factors in most models of the Heckscher-Ohlin theory therefore leaves few people happy. The problem, however, is that the introduction of even a homogeneous third factor seriously complicates the analysis. Even if this were to be incorporated successfully, however, the fact that 'land' in reality covers an immense variety of agricultural, forest and mineral resources remains a barrier to the application of simplified theoretical models for the explanation of actual trade flows. These problems have been discussed in chapter 4 in connexion with the 'availability' theory.

The lack of an adequate theoretical model has not, however, prevented empirical researchers from attempting to assess the possible influence of natural resource endowments on the Leontief Paradox. Although very abundantly endowed initially with these resources nearly a century of intensive industrialization and economic development may have made natural resources relatively scarce in the U.S. Hence the dominant influence on U.S. foreign trade may be the fact that she imports resource-intensive products to off-set this deficiency, exporting in return commodities which use both capital and labour relatively more intensively. By confining the analysis to only capital and labour the Leontief test may thus have dropped the most crucial dimension of the problem, coming up only with the finding that capital is used relatively more intensively than labour in imports whereas the more significant fact may be that *both* of these factors are used relatively less intensively as compared with natural resources.

Leontief's calculation, it may be recalled, excluded non-competitive imports such as coffee and certain minerals and other resource products totally unavailable in the U.S. In many other cases, however, where some limited domestic production of a commodity occurred, Leontief included it in his computations as a competitive import. It can reasonably be argued, however, that in these cases further domestic production to substitute for imports could not be undertaken at reasonable cost, because of the scarcity of the essential natural resources in the U.S. Hence they should be excluded from the calculation as non-competitive, even though some limited amount of local production takes place. In his later study Leontief did exclude these sectors and, interestingly enough, the Paradox disappeared with their exclusion. The capital-labour ratio in exports and imports was 10,110 dollars per man-year and 9270 dollars per man-year respectively, instead of the corresponding figures of 14,000 and 18,000 dollars per man-year respectively obtained earlier. Notice that in the U.S. these sectors are more capital-intensive than the average, so that their exclusion lowers the capital-labour ratio for both exports and imports significantly, but for imports proportionately more.

Another approach to the problem of the role of natural resources in the Leontief Paradox is adopted by J. Vanek (1963). He leaves the composition of exports and imports of the original Leontief test unchanged and tries to estimate the natural resource input per million dollars of exports and imports respectively, that is to bring in the missing third factor 'land'. Since it is impossible to measure directly the amount of 'land' used Vanek employs the plausible argument that the input of this factor is proportional to the natural resource *products* used, directly and indirectly as intermediate goods, per million dollars of exports and imports. The calculation of these resource product requirements of exports and imports can be made readily from Leontief's input-output data. Vanek found that 630,000 dollars worth of natural resource products is used per million dollars of import substitution whereas only 340,000 dollars worth is used per million dollars of export. Accepting this as an index of the amounts of 'land' used in each case, it can be seen that imports are more land-intensive than exports in the sense that both the land-labour and land-capital ratios are higher for imports than for exports.

Vanek also adduces some evidence that whereas there appears to be no significant relationship between labour and natural resource product input, there is evidence of complementarity between the latter and the input of capital. Hence his explanation of the Leontief Paradox is that it is the complementarity of capital with the true scarce factor 'land' that gives the appearance of imports being relatively more capital-intensive than exports.

In a Leontief-type study of Japanese foreign trade in 1955 S. Naya found that the capital-labour ratios were 395,000 yen per man-year and 236,000 yen per man-year in exports and competitive imports respectively (Naya, 1967). Since Japan's main source of comparative advantage is supposed to be her relatively plentiful supply of labour we once again obtain a paradox, but this time in the opposite direction. Excluding natural resource product sectors from the computation he found that the figures became 512,000 yen for exports and 520,000 yen for imports so that once again the paradox is removed. It is interesting to observe, however, that while natural resource products are capital-intensive in the U.S. they are labour-intensive in Japan, so that in both cases the result of excluding them is in the 'right' direction.

The influence of natural resources also explains similar paradoxes turned up by similar researches. Wahl found that

Canada's exports to the U.S. were more capital-intensive than her imports from that country, while Bharadwaj found that Indian bilateral trade with the U.S. exhibited a similar pattern of capital-intensive exports and labour-intensive imports (Wahl, 1961; Bharadwaj, 1962). The probable explanation of the Wahl finding is that mineral products, which are quite highly capital-intensive, figure largely in Canada's exports to the U.S. Agricultural commodities were an important Indian import from the U.S., and since the production of these commodities in India is by labour-intensive methods, this accounts for the Bharadwaj finding.

Human capital

Another significant explanation of the Leontief Paradox is in terms of the now fashionable concept of 'human capital', the investment in man that takes place through resources used for education and training of the labour force. Leontief in his second study, and also other investigators, found that there was a considerably higher average level of skill, and also of wages, in the export sectors than in the import replacement sectors. Both of these facts can be taken to reflect a greater quantity of human capital employed in the export sector. Hence if capital is defined as physical plus human capital it is quite possible that the relative factor-intensities of exports and imports will be reversed and the Paradox resolved.

The problem was tackled directly in an article by Kenen (1965). He takes wage differences between types of labour as being due to differences in investment in education and training and, using independently calculated estimates of the rate of return on such investments, he arrives at estimates of how much capital must have been invested in education and training to produce the observed difference in wages. Thus if the difference in wages between skilled and unskilled labour is 100 dollars and the rate of return on investment in education and training is 10 per cent, then 1000 dollars is the human capital invested in the skilled labour.

In his later study Leontief puts the physical capital per man-year in export and import-competing industries at 11·62 thousand dollars and 13·66 thousand dollars respectively. One of Kenen's alternative estimates of physical plus human capital is 30·61 thousand dollars for exports and 29·83 thousand dollars for import-competing industries. The Paradox is therefore removed, but only just.

Before leaving the subject of the Heckscher-Ohlin theory, however, the findings of one very interesting recent study should be reported. Moroney and Walker (1966) computed what they called 'location quotients' for a number of U.S. industries. These quotients are obtained by dividing *per capita* output of each industry in the South by *per capita* output of the same industry in the rest of the U.S. The greater this quotient the greater is the concentration of this industry in the South. Now it is widely believed that the South is more labour-abundant than the rest of the country. Hence they argued that on the basis of the Heckscher-Ohlin theory there should be a strong inverse correlation between the capital-labour ratios of a list of industries and their location quotients. This they did not find; instead there was even some evidence of the opposite tendency. They concluded that natural resources endowment patterns again overrode the capital-labour proportions as a determinant of specialization.

However, they also tested the hypothesis that there was an inverse correlation between capital-labour ratios and the percentage change in location quotients over time. They did find strong evidence in favour of this hypothesis. Thus although the Heckscher-Ohlin theory did not fit the pattern of specialization at a point of time it did explain the changes in that pattern over time. The theory could thus play a very fruitful role in the theory of economic development.

New Commodities and the 'R & D' Factor

One of the interesting novel approaches to the theory of international specialization discussed in chapter 4 was the idea that a country with a high level of *per capita* income and wages, such as the United States, would tend to have a comparative advantage in the production of new commodities, particularly in the fields of consumer durables and labour-saving producer goods. Industries in which there is a high rate of innovation in the form of introduction of a steady flow of new products would be characterized by a relatively high level of expenditure on 'R & D' (Research and Development). One would therefore expect that a ranking of U.S. industries in terms of their propensity to engage in R & D would be correlated with one based on degree of export competitiveness. Such a test has been conducted by Keesing (1967), with results that are very favourable to the hypothesis.

Keesing took a list of eighteen U.S. industries and compared the ranking of these on the basis of export competitiveness, which he measured by the proportion of U.S. exports to total Group of Ten exports, to a ranking based on the proportion of R & D personnel to total employment in each industry. A very high correlation was found. The data pertained to 1961 and 1962. Keesing reports that other measures of export competitiveness and R & D-intensity also show high correlations, but to a lesser extent. The choice of period does not apparently affect the result since both the measures used are quite stable over time. Similar favourable results linking R & D to U.S. exports were obtained in another study by Gruber, Mehta and Vernon (1967). Keesing also computed the 'research-intensiveness' of U.S. exports and imports, finding that 2·87 per cent of the labour force engaged in producing U.S. manufactured exports was engaged in R & D, while only 1·21 per cent of the labour force required to replace U.S. manufactured imports would be so engaged.

The very convincing evidence provided by these studies will doubtless be further refined and elaborated in future work. What will be of the greatest theoretical interest, however, is the explanation of what determines the propensity to engage in R & D itself. We have already come across some interesting hypotheses in this connexion but empirical evidence is as yet lacking. It would seem that a commodity by commodity 'case study' approach would be particularly useful here as an essential preliminary before any broad generalizations can be made with confidence.

6 The Gains from Trade

The questions of international trade theory considered so far in this book have all been concerned with the 'positive' part of the subject, the derivation and testing of theorems about the nature and effects of the pattern of international trade. The question of the nature of the benefit or 'gains' that countries obtain, individually and as a whole, from engaging in international trade has so far been avoided. We have only inquired into the conditions that lead to trade, and the nature of that trade. The question of 'gains', however, lay at the heart of the classical economists' pioneering contributions to the subject. These contributions were not made in a spirit of aloof objective 'scientific' inquiry but as partisan arguments in favour of the repeal of agricultural protection in England – the famous debate on the 'Corn Laws'. In this debate the 'welfare' question was paramount – would England be better off or not if the Corn Laws were repealed?

An answer to this question necessarily involves the establishment of some criterion by which the effects of the repeal could be evaluated and compared to strike a net balance in favour or against. 'Value judgements' must be made. Prior to the application of normative criteria to assess the effects of the measure, however, positive analysis needs to be used to ascertain the nature of the effects themselves. Thus before answering the question of whether countries will gain or lose by engaging in trade between themselves we must know the conditions under which trade will arise, and the pattern of that trade. Although Ricardo, Torrens and the other early classical economists considered the welfare question of paramount interest they were not able to solve its satisfactorily, by modern standards.

Their great achievement was really in the sphere of positive economics – in the formulation of the theory of comparative advantage which, as we have seen in the last chapter, leads to propositions that are capable of being empirically tested.

In this final chapter we shall present the essentials of the modern theory of the welfare aspect of international trade, or the 'gains from trade' as it has come to be called. It will be instructive to begin, however, with a brief examination of the classical approach to this problem, to see how the modern doctrine has evolved in response to its inadequancies.[3]

The Classical Approach

The Ricardian approach to the gains from trade can be illustrated by means of Figure 19 in which the line *AB* indicates the different combination of two goods *X* and *Y* which a country can produce, the total quantity of labour available and the fixed input of labour per unit of each commodity being given. Suppose now that the country has the opportunity to trade at terms represented by the slope of the line *CB*. It can now devote all its resources to production of *OB* units of *X* and trade along *CB*. The equilibrium consumption point without trade would be somewhere on *AB*, whereas it would be somewhere on *CB* if trade is engaged in. It could therefore be said that the gain from trade consists of the enlargement of consumption possibilities that is now open to the community for the same input of labour. This proposition can be taken to illustrate the well-known statement of Ricardo that while 'no extension of foreign trade will immediately increase the amount of value [by which he meant the total input of labour in a country] nevertheless it will very powerfully contribute to increase the mass of commodities, and therefore, the sum of enjoyments.'

Malthus attributed to Ricardo, questionably in the opinion of Professor Viner, the view that the gain from trade consisted in the saving of cost resulting from obtaining the imported

3. See Viner (1937, ch. 9) for a very interesting commentary on the classical theory of the gains from trade.

goods through trade instead of by domestic production. Thus let *e* be the equilibrium point on *AB* in the absence of trade and *f* the equilibrium point on *CB* under free trade. If the combination of *X* and *Y* represented by *f* were to be produced domestically, the input of labour will have to increase sufficiently to push

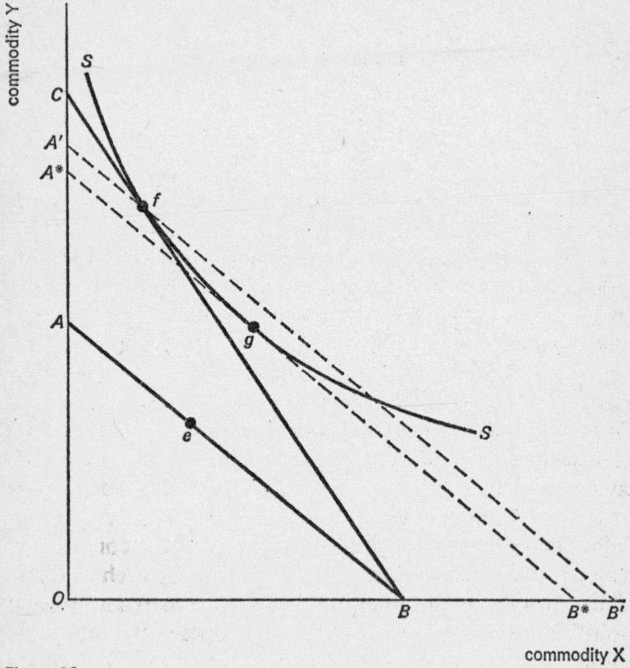

Figure 19

the production-possibilities curve *AB* out to *A′B′*, the gain from trade being measured by *BB′*/*OB*.

Always more conscious of the consumption side of a problem than his great rival Malthus asserted that Ricardo's cost approach greatly over-estimated the gains from trade. His criticism can be paraphrased as pointing out that if the domestic production-possibility curve were to shift out to *A ′B′* then *f* would not be the equilibrium point. Relative prices along

A′B′ would be more favourable to the exported commodity *X* than along *CB*, so that consumers will prefer a point to the right of *f* on *A′B′* to *f* itself. Hence we cannot say that the gain from the opportunity to trade along *CB* is equivalent to an expansion of labour input in the proportion *BB′*/*OB* in terms of its effect on consumer welfare, since the latter change is preferable. The measure attributed to Ricardo would therefore over-state the gains from trade.

The Ricardian measure can be modified to take account of this criticism, however, by taking, instead of the amount of labour needed to produce the free trade equilibrium combination of goods consumed, the amount of labour needed to produce a closed economy equilibrium combination that is equivalent to *f* in terms of consumer welfare. This solution, however, raises the problem of how to define alternative combinations of goods to be equivalent in terms of the welfare of a group – the problem of 'community indifference curves'. The first rigorous construction of such curves was in an article by T. Scitovsky (1942). For a community of *n* individuals a *Scitovsky curve* is constructed by taking the minimum amount of one good that is necessary to keep all *n* individuals each at a prescribed level of indifference for himself, given the total amount of the other good available. This definition implies that each combination of goods on a Scitovsky curve is allocated optimally between the members of the community, given the level of satisfaction to be enjoyed by each of them. It can readily be seen that this requires the marginal rates of substitution between the goods, or the slopes of the individual indifference curves, to be the same for all members of the community at their respective consumption points, since otherwise a re-allocation of the same total combination could make it possible to keep all individuals at their prescribed levels of satisfaction and still have some of one good left over.

In Figure 19 let *SS* denote the Scitovsky curve corresponding to the levels of welfare enjoyed by each individual at the free trade equilibrium point *f*. The point *g* on *SS* will make each individual as well off as he is under free trade if, instead of the opportunity to trade, the labour input of the community rose sufficiently to push the production-possibilities curve out to A^*B^*. The gain from trade would therefore correspond to BB^*/OB instead of the larger BB'/OB.

A logically equivalent alternative approach is to draw the Scitovsky curve (not shown in the diagram) corresponding to the closed economy equilibrium point *e*. A tangent to this curve with slope equal to that of *CB*, the terms on which the opportunity to trade exists, could then be drawn and the point B'', this time to the left of *B*, at which this tangent cuts the horizontal axis can be determined. BB'' thus represents the reduction in labour input that the economy could sustain, and still maintain the same level of welfare for everybody by taking advantage of the opportunity to trade. BB''/OB would thus again be a measure of the gains from trade.

Some limitations of the classical approach, labour as the only scarce factor of production and fixed technical coefficients, can readily be removed. The straight line production-possibility curve *AB* can be replaced by one concave to the origin derived from the two-factor, variable coefficients box diagram as described in chapter 2, without the argument being affected in any way. The shifts in the production-possibility curves that are equivalent in welfare terms to the opportunity to trade, however, require to be interpreted as 'neutral' shifts, that is as the result of expansion of both factors in the same proportion or of technical progress in the two sectors taking place at the same rate. The problem of the gains from trade is therefore made logically equivalent to that of the 'gains from growth'. In view of all the attention that the gains from trade have received in the literature of economics, it is surprising that so little has been devoted to the sense in which an economy that experiences growth can be said to improve its welfare. Population change makes this latter problem even more ambiguous than that of the gains from trade in a static context.

A much more serious limitation, however, is the assumption that has to be made about the distribution of income. In order to obtain a measure of the gains from trade in terms of the equivalent production expansion or economy in resources that it makes possible, the welfare levels of all individuals in either the pre-trade or post-trade equilibrium situation have to be taken as given. The point, however, is that trade is bound to change the welfare positions of most individuals, and not in the same direction for all of them. The Stolper-Samuelson theorem tells us, for example, that individuals who derive their income wholly or predominantly from the relatively scarce factor will be harmed by trade. Thus, if trade makes some people better off and others worse off, in what sense can the welfare of the community as a whole be said to be greater as a result of trade?

A Digression on Welfare Economics

An answer to this question is only possible in terms of modern welfare economics, developed since the late thirties by Kaldor, Hicks, Scitovsky, Samuelson and others.[4] The criterion proposed by Kaldor and Hicks was that even if some people lose as a result of a change, the repeal of the Corn Laws for example, it would still be possible to say that the welfare of the community as a whole had increased if it were possible for the gainers to compensate the losers and still be better off themselves. The question of whether compensation should in fact be given is taken as a matter of ethics, on which economics can make no pronouncement. Hence the concept of welfare used is *potential* welfare, that is welfare has increased if we *could* reach, if we wanted to, a situation where no one is worse off and someone at least is better off. The Kaldor-Hicks 'compensation principle' was, however, shown to have a serious weakness by Scitovsky. He pointed out that is quite possible for situation A to be better than situation B on the Kaldor-Hicks test and also for B to be better than A by the same test, that is while the gainers could compensate the losers after the change, it could also be true that the losers could compensate the gainers if the *status quo* was restored.

The 'compensation principle' can be clarified considerably by the use of a diagram invented by Samuelson called the 'utility-possibility' curve. In Figure 20 let $U°U°$ show the

4. See Mishan (1960) for an account of this development.

maximum level of utility (in terms of his own preferences) that one person can enjoy given the level of utility to be enjoyed by the other member of a community of two. The fact that goods are scarce means that the more well off we make the one, the less well off must be the other, which accounts for the slope of $U°U°$ being everywhere negative. The analogy between $U°U°$ and a production-possibility curve is obvious, hence its name. Suppose that the initial welfare enjoyed by the two persons correspond to the point A inside $U°U°$. Now a certain change occurs shifting the welfare point to B, above and to the left of A and on $U°U°$. Since one is better off and the other worse

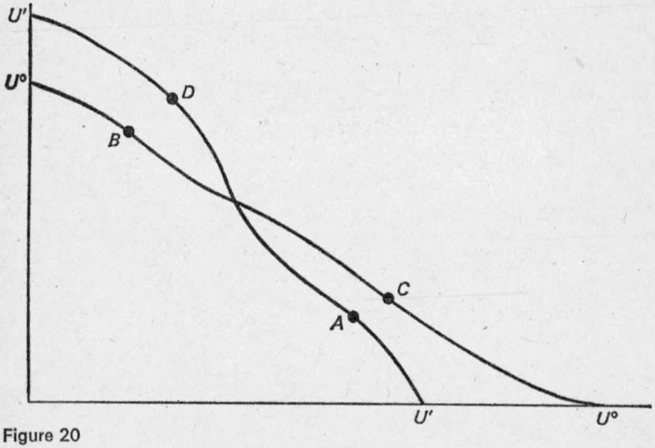

Figure 20

off we cannot immediately say that the welfare of the community as a whole is raised. But, by applying the compensation principle we can say that by a redistribution of the scarce goods we could move from B to C, where both are better off than in the original situation A. Hence it can be said that the change increases potential welfare.

As Scitovsky pointed out it is quite possible for the utility-possibility curve $U'U'$ on which A is located, which shows the level of potential welfare attainable with the collection of goods available in the original situation, to pass outside of B, so that the point *D* for example makes both persons better off than at *B*. We are obviously confounded if we have to say that *B* is both better and worse than *A* on the Kaldor-Hicks compensation test. Scitovsky proposed that the Kaldor-Hicks test should be applied *twice* before we can say that an increase in welfare has occurred by a movement from *A* to *B*. The first condition is that *B* must be better than *A* on the Kaldor-Hicks test and the second is that *A* must *not* be better than *B* on this same test. Samuelson, however, showed that even the Scitovsky test is unsatisfactory, since in Figure 21 we find that although *B* is better than *A* on the double Scitovsky criterion there is a point

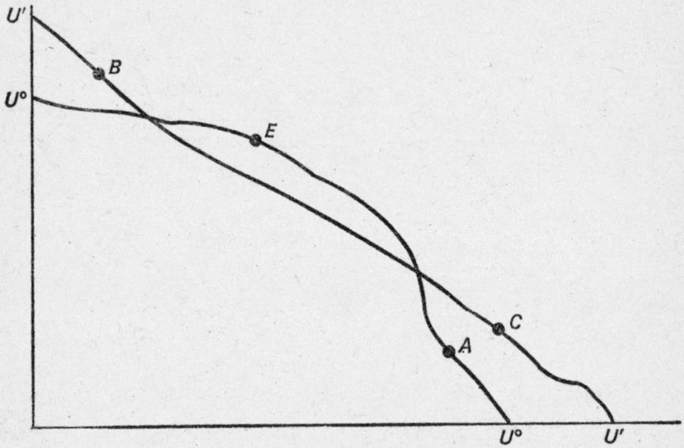

Figure 21

E attainable prior to the change which is not attainable after. Hence Samuelson argues that the only complete test for whether welfare has increased is for the utility-possibility curve after the change to be *nowhere inside* the corresponding curve before the change and at least somewhere outside it. In other words every welfare position attainable before the change must be attainable after, together with at least one position that was not attainable before.

The Samuelson criterion naturally makes us think of trying to push the utility-possibility curve corresponding to any given economic situation out as far as possible, that is given the conditions on the availability of goods to maximize the welfare of one individual given the welfare to be enjoyed by the other. A situation in which it is impossible to increase the welfare of one individual without decreasing that of another is termed 'Pareto-optimal' after the great pioneer of modern welfare economics. We shall now state briefly the conditions for Pareto-optimality.

We take as given the amounts of productive factors available, the technology of transforming inputs into the different outputs and the preferences of each individual with regard to the ranking of alternative sets of consumption goods. In terms of the standard geometric tools these assumptions amount to taking as given the box diagram of production and the indifference curve systems of all individuals.

It is easy to see that an essential condition for Pareto-optimality is for the economy to produce on the transformation or production-possibilities curve since otherwise a change is feasible that will provide more of all goods and so enable us to raise the welfare of everybody in the community. As was seen in chapter 2 this requires that the marginal rate of substitution between the inputs must be equal in the production of both the outputs. Equality in the marginal rates of substitution between any pair of inputs in the production of all outputs is thus one essential condition for Pareto-optimality.

Given any point on the transformation curve, which determines the set of goods available for consumption, we need to distribute this set of goods efficiently over all consumers. It should not be possible, by shifting the goods between the individuals, to make anyone better off without making someone else worse off. Suppose, for example, that the marginal rate of substitution in consumption of individual A is 3 units of commodity X for 1 unit of commodity Y while for B it is $2X$ for $1Y$. Then if $1Y$ is transferred from B to A and $2X$ from A to B, we observe that B is indifferent whereas A is better off since $1Y$ is worth $3X$ to him whereas he only loses $2X$ in exchange for $1Y$. Hence equality in the marginal rates of substitution in consumption for any pair of goods for all individuals is a second essential condition for Pareto-optimality.

Suppose that a collection of goods determined by a point on the transformation curve is distributed efficiently and that the common marginal rate of substitution for all individuals is 2*X* for 1 *Y*. The slope of the transformation curve at the point in question, or marginal rate of transformation is, let us say, 3*X* for 1 *Y*. It follows that Pareto-optimality is not achieved since if 1 less *Y* were produced and 3 more *X* were substituted in production, any individual whose consumption of *Y* was reduced by that 1 unit could be adequately compensated by 2

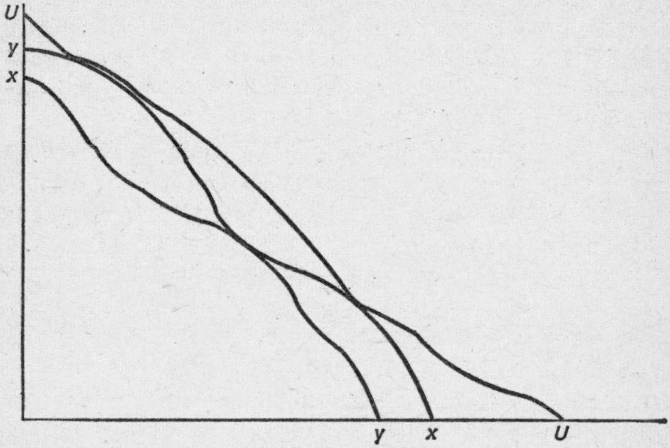

Figure 22

more *X* whereas 3 is available. Hence what is known as the 'consumer's sovereignty' condition is also essential for Pareto-optimality – the marginal rate of transformation in production for any pair of goods must be equal to the common marginal rate of substitution in consumption for all individuals.

In Figure 22 the curves *xx* and *yy* denote the utility-possibility curves corresponding to *particular points* on the production-possibilities curve. Hence only the first two conditions for Pareto-optimality are satisfied at all points on each of these curves. The utility-possibility curve *UU* corresponding to all three conditions for Pareto-optimality is obtained by taking the 'outer envelope' of the infinity of curves such as *xx* and *yy* drawn for each point on the production-possibility curve. Thus with the given resources, technology and tastes, *UU* marks the boundary of potential welfare for the community *in the absence of any opportunity to engage in external trade.*

It is easy to see that if more inputs were available or if more output could be obtained per unit of input the curve *UU* would be shifted outwards at all points. Certain other changes may enable more of one good to be produced but less of another, for example, a dam may enable the production of more manufactured goods as a result of a boost to electric power facilities while as a result of its construction cultivable land is flooded and agricultural production is consequently reduced. In this case *UU* would be *twisted*, moving out for part of the way and in for another.

What effect will the opportunity to engage in external trade have on *UU*? The answer to this question is essentially the modern answer to the question of what are the gains from trade. One important distinction that must be made is between the gains from trade as seen from the cosmopolitan view-point of the welfare of the world as a whole and from the nationalistic viewpoint of a single country. Each of these cases is analysed below.

Trade and Welfare: Cosmopolitan Viewpoint

In chapter 2 it was shown how the terms of trade and export-import volumes that would prevail in competitive international equilibrium would be determined. In the present section the welfare aspect of domestic and international equilibrium will be considered.

Given the factor endowments, technology and tastes for each country and assuming perfect competition, it is easy to see that the conditions of Pareto-optimality will be met in each country in the absence of any international trade. Because of perfect competition, factor prices facing all industries must be the same everywhere and in the endeavour to minimize costs, the marginal rates of substitution between inputs in production will be equated to the common factor price-ratio and hence to each other. All consumers will face the same product prices and since the marginal rates of substitution in consumption for each individual are equated to the product price-ratios for utility maximization, they will all be equal to each other. Finally the equilibrium level of outputs will be such that the price-ratio between products will be equal to their relative marginal costs or marginal rate of transformation between them, and with producers and consumers facing the same prices, this means that the marginal rate of transformation between commodities in production is equal to the common marginal rate of substitution between them in the consumption of all individuals. Hence all three conditions of Pareto-optimality will be satisfied.

Suppose now that the countries, instead of each being treated as an isolated economic system, are viewed as forming a single 'world economy'. Then it is clear that the allocation of resources in the world economy is not Pareto-optimal. The reason is that the domestic closed-economy equilibrium prices will generally differ between the countries in the absence of trade so that marginal rates of transformation in production and substitution in consumption will also differ from country to country with the result that none of the Pareto conditions will be satisfied for the world economy as a whole.

Let free international trade under conditions of perfect competition be opened up and, at once, the situation changes. In the absence of transport costs the same prices for all goods must exist in all countries, those corresponding to the international equilibrium level at which exports and imports of each commodity exactly balance. This implies that marginal rates of transformation in production and substitution in consumption will be equal everywhere. Thus the second and third conditions for Pareto-optimality will be satisfied. What about the first? Unless the stringent conditions for international factor-price equalization exist factor prices, and hence marginal rates of substitution between factors in production, will not be the same from country to country. If it is assumed that factors of production do not move at all across national boundaries, as is generally done in the pure theory of international trade, then these differences in factor prices will not be wiped out by factor movements from country to country.

Although the condition that marginal rates of substitution between factors in production must be equalized cannot be met, production in the world economy under free trade is clearly efficient in the sense that, given the level of world output for one good, the level of the other is maximized under the constraints of technological knowledge, factor supply and factor *location*. In other words production under free trade takes place on the boundary of the world transformation curve, the manner of construction of which was explained in chapter 2. Of course if it were possible to shift factors between countries then points beyond the boundary would also become feasible, but since this is not the case the best results possible under the given conditions are obtained along the boundary of the world transformation curve. Under autarky the marginal rates of transformation in production are different, say $3X$ for $1Y$ in country A and $2X$ for $1Y$ in country B. Hence if A produces 1 less Y and 3 more X and B 1 more Y and 2 less X, then the production of Y in the world would be the same, whereas that of X has increased by 1 unit, without there being any international movement of factors. One of the great advantages of free trade is thus the fact that it makes world production efficient in the sense defined. If the conditions of the factor price equalization theorem were to hold then marginal rates of substitution between factors would be the same all over the world, and hence the full set of Pareto conditions would be met without the necessity of any international factor movements.

Since free trade also makes it possible for marginal rates of substitution in consumption to be the same everywhere, and for the common marginal rate of transformation in production to be equated to this common marginal rate of substitution in consumption, it follows that the welfare situation under free trade in the world economy is such that no individual can be made better off without someone else in the world (not necessarily in the same country) being made worse off. Suppose that there are N individuals in the world and that the welfare of each of $(N-2)$ of them is fixed at some arbitrary level. Then we can construct a utility-possibility curve in two dimensions, as in Figure 23, to show the maximum level of welfare that can be enjoyed by one of the remaining individuals given the level to be enjoyed by the other. Under free trade the welfare position of the two individuals will be somewhere on the curve *UU* in Figure 23, say at the point *F*.

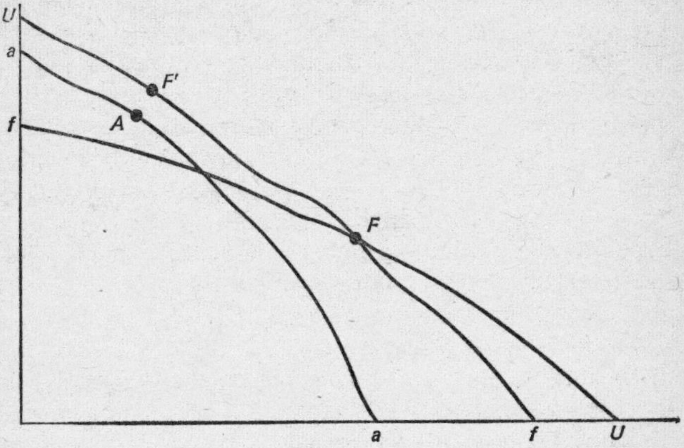

Figure 23

The exact sense in which free trade is superior to no trade or restricted trade requires careful consideration. Although free trade will lead to a point on *UU*, it does not follow that at that particular point both individuals must necessarily be better off than under no trade. In Figure 23 this is shown by *F* being to the right of but below the no trade welfare point *A*. Furthermore, the utility-possibility curve corresponding to the actual free trade equilibrium combination of goods may pass below *A*, so that no redistribution of this set of goods also can be unambiguously superior to *A*. What is true is that there is always *some* free trade equilibrium point on *UU*, such as *F'*, which is definitely superior to *A*. In principle, it is possible to move the free trade equilibrium welfare position from *F* to *F'* by a system of lump-sum taxes and transfers, that maintain the Pareto conditions intact, while shifting the pattern of production and consumption in the desired direction. In practice, however, any scheme of income redistribution is likely to violate the Pareto conditions in some way. The utility-possibility curve *aa* corresponding to the no trade combination of goods of course lies within *UU* throughout since the Pareto conditions are not met along it.

Suppose that the two individuals whose welfare is plotted in Figure 23 come from different countries, one of them a 'representative citizen' of a rich or advanced country and the other of a poor or under-developed country. Starting at *F* the under-developed country may impose a tariff, the effect of which is to turn the terms of trade in its favour and hence to increase the welfare of its citizens. The citizens of the rich country must consequently be harmed. The new welfare point cannot be on *UU* since the tariff will prevent the international equalization of marginal rates of transformation and substitution. The point *A* can serve to illustrate the new welfare position.

This violation of free trade can be justified on the grounds that it improves the welfare of poor citizens of the world at the expense of rich ones and that such a change is desirable ethically. However, it can be pointed out that a superior solution to the problem of raising the welfare of poor citizens of poor countries is possible. This is to redistribute income by the system of lump-sum taxes and transfers, mentioned previously, in such a way that a point like *F′* is reached in which the welfare of both types of citizens is higher under free trade than under the tariff point *A*. In short, foreign aid in the form of outright transfers to poor countries financed by lump-sum taxes in rich countries is always a more efficient way of redistributing income internationally than unilateral trade restrictions by under-developed countries. Needless to say trade redistrictions practised by advanced countries against under-developed countries are doubly undesirable since, in addition to leading to inefficiencies in production and consumption, they also redistribute income in the 'wrong' direction.

Trade and Welfare: Nationalistic Viewpoint

In this section the viewpoint adopted towards the question of the gains from trade is the nationalistic one of a single country rather than the cosmopolitan one of the welfare of the world economy as a whole. It is this aspect of the problem of the gains from trade that has received most attention in the literature. The modern treatment of the subject stems from a famous article by Samuelson (1939). The analysis is considerably simplified by using the utility-possibility curve as a tool which, however, was not introduced until 1950, again by Samuelson (1950). In a more recent paper Samuelson (1964) uses the instrument he forged in 1950 for the problem he solved in 1939, and it is this second article of his that is the basis for this section. Reference should also be made to articles by Baldwin (1952) and Kemp (1964).

In the world economy as a whole production and consumption of every commodity must necessarily be equal if there is no change in stocks. Hence what we may call the world 'consumption-possibility' curve, showing the alternative combinations of goods that it is possible to consume, coincides with the world production-possibility curve. The world as a whole is a closed economy. For a single country in a trading world, however, consumption-possibilities and production-possibilities are not the same since imports can increase the availability of a good for consumption and exports will decrease it. For the welfare optimum of a trading economy we must first determine the consumption-possibility curve as the basis for the Pareto-optimal utility-possibility curve.

If the terms of trade facing a country are taken as fixed then Figure 24 indicates the shape of the consumption-possibilities curve. The curve *CC* shows the maximum amount of *Y* that it is possible for the society to consume given its consumption of *X*. The slope of *CC* is equal to the fixed terms of trade. Any point on *CC* is reached by producing the combination of *X* and *Y* determined by the point *Z*, and then moving along *CC* to the desired point by exporting one good and importing the other.

Suppose, however, that instead of the opportunity to trade being given at fixed terms of trade (constant world prices for all commodities), it is given in the form of the reciprocal supply and demand curve or offer curve of the trading partner, showing how much of one commodity it is willing to export or import in exchange for a specific amount of the other. The trading partner's offer curve marks the most favourable trade bargains that are open to the home country. If it wants to squeeze the maximum advantage from trade, it can in principle manipulate

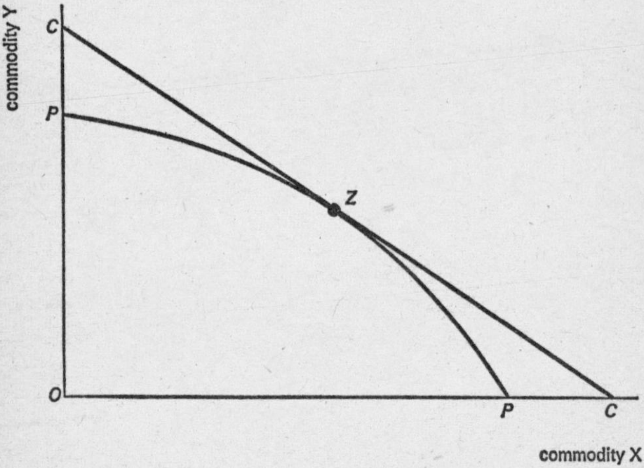

Figure 24

its commercial policy (tariffs, quotas, etc.) so as to force the equilibrium trading point to that point on the partner's offer curve which is most favourable to itself (the home country). In this case the terms of trade would not be fixed but would depend on the point on the foreign offer curve at which the home country chooses to trade. In effect the home country in this case is a monopolist of its export commodity, the foreign offer curve playing the role of the consumer demand curve in the traditional theory of monopoly. The construction of the consumption-possibilities curve is now somewhat more complicated but can nevertheless be accomplished as follows.

Consider any set of arbitrary combinations of *X* and *Y* that are produced, traded and consumed. This set must of course be such that the amount consumed of each commodity is equal to production plus imports or minus exports. Keeping the amount of *X* consumed fixed we may inquire whether or not it is possible to increase the consumption of *Y* by some adjustment to production and trade. Suppose that at the arbitrary point at which we start the slope of the production-possibilities curve is 2 *Y* for 1 *X*, and that the slope of the foreign offer curve is 3 *Y* for 1 *X*. Let us call these slopes PTR (production transformation rate) and TTR (trade transformation rate) respectively. For the given magnitudes of these slopes it is easy to see how it is possible to increase the consumption of *Y* without reducing that of *X*. Let 1 more unit of *X* be produced and exported in exchange for 3 units of *Y*. Home production of *Y* will fall by 2 units but since imports increase by 3 units the consumption of *Y* will go up by 1 unit. *X* consumption will remain the same since the additional production of *X* is exported. A little reflection will show that such a result can always be achieved whenever PTR $\neq$ TTR. The condition for *Y* consumption to be a maximum for any given level of *X* consumption is therefore that PTR = TTR. At the margin the opportunity cost of 1 unit of *Y* must be the same whether it is obtained through domestic production or foreign trade.

With this principle in mind the construction of the consumption-possibility curve can proceed quite easily. In Figure 25 *ROR′* is the foreign offer curve. If the origin of the domestic production-possibility curve is placed at a point *P* on *ROR′* then the point *S* on the production-possibility curve, where its slope is equal to that of *ROR′* at *P*, is also a point on the consumption-possibility curve with origin at *O*. Consumption of *X* is equal to *SR* which is production *QS* less export *QR*. Consumption of *Y* is equal to *SU*, which is production *ST* plus import *TU*. The point *S* must therefore lie on the consumption-possibility curve since both the principle of equal cost at the margin and the condition that consumption of each good is equal to production plus export or minus import are met.

Given that consumption of X is equal to OU the maximum amount of Y that can be consumed is SU and vice versa. How are the other points on the consumption-possibility curve to be obtained? In exactly the same manner but by placing the origin of the production-possibilities curve at different points along ROR'. By sliding the origin of the production-possibilities curve along ROR', and marking the point on this curve where its slope is equal to that of ROR' at the point where it is touched by the origin, we can trace out the locus of all points on the consumption-possibility curve as the line CC in the

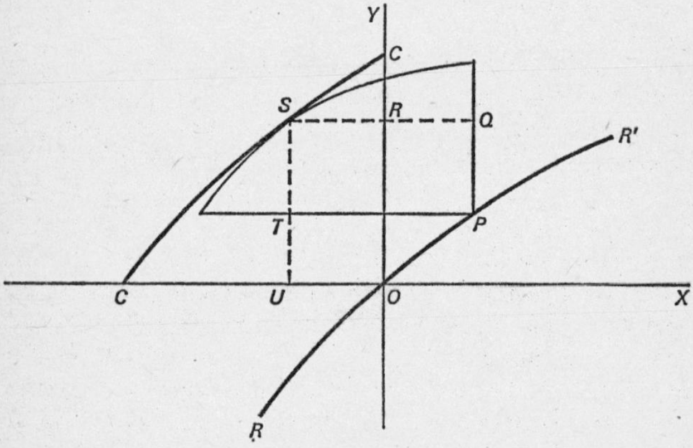

Figure 25

diagram. CC is the 'envelope curve' to the successive segments of the production-possibilities curve that lies in the upper left-hand quadrant as the origin travels along ROR'. Since this technique was first used by Baldwin the curve CC is usually referred to in the literature as the 'Baldwin envelope' (Baldwin, 1948).

When the origin of the production-possibilities curve is placed at O the point where its slope is equal to that of ROR' will also lie on the Baldwin envelope. All other points on the curve will lie *within* the Baldwin envelope. Hence the consumption-possibilities curve with trading opportunities given in the form of a foreign offer curve enclose the consumption-possibilities curve without trading opportunities, which is the production-possibilities curve itself. The situation is therefore similar to that of Figure 24, where fixed terms of trade are assumed, except that the Baldwin envelope is not linear. In fact the linear curve *CC* in Figure 24 is a special case of the Baldwin envelope which arises when the foreign offer curve *ROR′* in Figure 25 is a straight line. Since the slope of *ROR′* in this case is constant there is only one optimum point on the production-possibilities curve, where its slope is equal to that of *ROR′*. The term Baldwin envelope will henceforth be used for the consumption-possibilities curves of both Figures 24 and 25.

Each point on the Baldwin envelope can generate a utility-possibility curve along which the utility of one individual is maximized, given the utility of the other and the availability of goods as determined by the fixed point on the envelope. Along each of these curves the Pareto condition that the marginal rates of substitution in consumption are the same for both individuals is satisfied. However there is always the opportunity to do better by changing the combination of goods available for allocation. This opportunity will arise whenever the marginal rate of substitution in consumption is different from the marginal rate of transformation, which is equal to the slope of the Baldwin envelope. Hence the true outermost frontier of welfare for the society will be obtained by drawing the utility-possibility curves corresponding to each point on the Baldwin envelope in turn, and then taking the outer envelope of all of them. Along this utility-possibility envelope the marginal rate of transformation of one good into another (through trade and production) will be equal to the marginal rates of substitution in consumption.

As has already been described a utility-possibility envelope can be constructed from the production-possibilities curve by itself. This envelope is the welfare frontier of society in the absence of the opportunity to trade. What will be the relationship between the two welfare frontiers for the society? It is apparent that the welfare frontier with trade will lie entirely outside the closed economy frontier, except at one common point corresponding to the combination of goods determined by the common point of the production-possibilities curve and the Baldwin envelope. The opportunity to engage in trade thus increases the welfare of the community in the strict Samuelson sense that it shifts out the utility-possibility curve in such a way that all welfare positions attainable previously are still attainable, plus some more. The gains from trade, in modern doctrine, is nothing other than this fact – whatever the original welfare position under autarky, there exists a position with trade such that all individuals are better off. Samuelson has summed up the situation with the pithy dictum that 'some trade is better than no trade'. But which trade is best? In other words, how can the optimum levels of consumption, production and trade of each good be determined?

The answer to this question obviously depends on the point that is chosen on the welfare frontier corresponding to the Baldwin envelope. The selection of this point must be arbitrary since the relative well-being to be enjoyed by different individuals is an ethical question. Given the selection of a point on the welfare frontier as 'best' in terms of some criterion of social welfare that weighs the relative deservingness of the individuals against each other, the problem of what consumption, production and trade pattern will make this welfare position attainable is readily solved. The individual indifference curves corresponding to the optimum welfare point can be combined into a Scitovsky community indifference curve and drawn in the upper left-hand quadrant of Figure 25. This curve must be attainable by a point on the Baldwin envelope since the original welfare point from which it was derived is a feasible one. Furthermore no point on the Baldwin envelope can lie above this curve since the original welfare point is a point on the frontier. Hence the Scitovsky curve must be tangential to the Baldwin envelope at one point, say S. The optimum consumption, production and trade levels of each good can now be read off Figure 25.

The modified Ricardian measure of the gains from trade introduced earlier can be applied in the present situation. The minimum rate of 'neutral' expansion needed to reach the

Scitovsky curve tangential to the Baldwin envelope at *S*, in the absence of trade, can be ascertained and the gains from trade equated to this 'welfare-equivalent' expansion in productive capacity. However, the result will always vary with the point that is selected as optimum on the welfare frontier so that there will be one 'cardinal' measure of the gains from trade for each possible optimum point on the welfare frontier. Given the welfare point, however, a unique cardinal measurement of the gains from trade is always possible in principle by the method described.

The exact sense in which 'some trade is better than no trade' needs to be carefully defined since it is open to misunderstanding. In Figure 26 the utility-possibility curve *TT* is the welfare frontier with trade, while *AA* is the welfare frontier under autarky. Each of these curves is an envelope of curves corresponding to fixed combinations of goods, such as *tt* and *aa*. Suppose that *M* on *aa* is the optimum point under autarky and *N* on *tt* is the optimum point with trade. It is perfectly possible for *M* not to be attainable by redistribution of income along *tt*, so that the trading optimum is not necessarily better than the autarky optimum when the *fixed combinations* of goods available at each point are considered. By changing the combination of goods available however, that is by moving along *TT* instead of *tt*, it is always possible to find a superior solution to *M* with trade. This is the sense in which 'some trade is better than no trade' is to be understood.

The next problem to consider is the important one of the relationship between optimum trade, as determined above, and free trade. It is easily seen that *no* free trade equilibrium point can be on the Baldwin envelope, and hence free trade can never be optimal since any optimum combination of goods must lie on this envelope. To see this let the point *P* in Figure 27 denote a free trade equilibrium position, that is suppose that domestic demand is such that in the absence of any restrictions on trade the domestic offer curve cuts the foreign offer curve at *P*. The terms of trade will therefore be determined by the slope of the line *OP*. The marginal rate of transformation in production must also be equal to the slope of *OP* under free trade. It follows that the production point on the transformation curve cannot be at the otimum point *S* since the slope there is equal to the slope of the foreign offer curve at *P*, which is not equal to the slope of *OP*. Hence the marginal rates of transformation through production and trade are not equal under free trade, which is therefore non-optimal from the nationalistic point of view of the domestic economy.

The optimum point *S* on the Baldwin envelope could be attained directly, if there is some form of state regulation or planning of trade and production, or through a suitable tariff

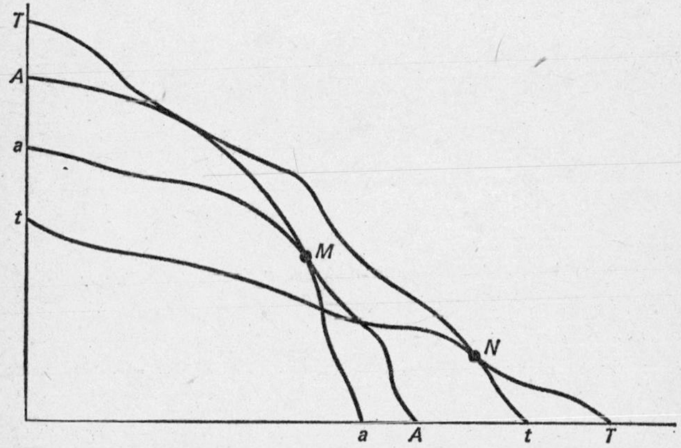

Figure 26

policy if market forces alone are to be relied upon. A tariff on imports which raises the relative price of imports and exports to domestic producers and consumers to equality with the slope of the foreign offer curve at *S*, instead of equality with the terms of trade *OP*, will secure the optimum position and is hence referred to as an 'optimum tariff' (Graaf, 1957, ch.9). It is clear that the level of the optimum tariff depends not only on the slope of the foreign offer curve, but also on the choice of the optimum point on the Baldwin envelope which in turn depends on the point selected on the welfare frontier.

Although free trade is never optimal, except in the special

case when the foreign offer curve is a straight line, it can be shown that 'free trade is better than no trade' in the same sense that some trade is better than none. In Figure 27 let the point *A* on the transformation curve denote the optimum production and consumption point under autarky. The point *P* on the foreign offer curve will be a point of free trade equilibrium if demand conditions at home are suitably adjusted. The point *O* on the transformation curve is the production point, and *OG* is the domestic export of commodity *X*, and *PG* the

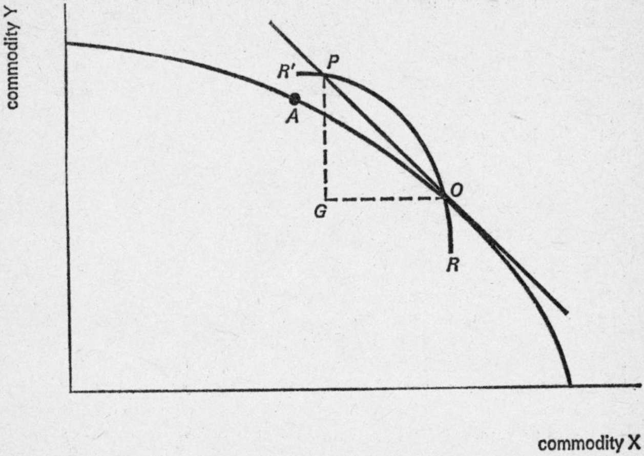

Figure 27

domestic import of commodity *Y*. Since at *P* more of both commodities is available than at *A* it follows that it is possible to make everybody better off under free trade than under no trade. Any particular free trade equilibrium point is of course not necessarily better than the autarky equilibrium point, as the argument of Figure 26 shows, but there is always some free trade point which is better.

In discussing the welfare implications of trade it has so far been assumed that there are no impediments to the smooth functioning of the price mechanism. There is a large and growing body of research, however, that examines the consequences of various imperfections or impediments to the smooth working of the price mechanism – such factors as increasing returns to scale, external economies and diseconomies, monopoly and so on. The superiority of free trade to no trade is no longer certain in these cases and situations can arise in which free trade is definitely worse than no trade. A full treatment of all these cases cannot be attempted here, but one problem will be analysed in some detail as an illustration of the type of outcome that is possible whenever there is a departure from the usual framework of assumptions.

Suppose that the factors of production are completely immobile between the different sectors of the economy, which is the opposite of the usual assumption that there is perfect mobility. Will this alone overthrow the superiority of some trade to no trade? In Figure 28 the transformation curve has become the rectangle *OADB* with *OA* being the production of Y and *OB* the production of X. This is because it is assumed that it is impossible to produce any other combination due to the complete immobility of the factors of production. Suppose now that trade is possible either at fixed terms of trade denoted by the slope of *TT′* as in Figure 28 or at terms determined by a given foreign offer curve. The effect is clearly to enlarge the consumption-possibility region from that bounded by *OADB* to that bounded by *OTT′*. Hence the welfare frontier corresponding to autarky will lie within that corresponding to trade, except at one point where they will coincide. Thus the result that some trade is superior to no trade continues to be true, in spite of the removal of the assumption of perfect mobility. The economy is unable to alter its production pattern to specialize in the direction indicated by the opportunity to trade, but it is able to alter its consumption pattern in ways that were impossible before, and this widens the welfare possibilities open to the community.

Let it now be further assumed that in addition to all factors being completely immobile that labour in both sectors will not accept a real wage lower than what it is currently earning in terms of commodity Y. Since there is no labour mobility the earnings in terms of Y in the two sectors need not be the same.

Suppose that when trade is opened up the price of X falls relatively to the price of Y which is the exported commodity. Since the production point does not change as a result of trade the marginal physical productivities of labour in both sectors will remain unchanged. Labour in Y production will thus earn the same amount of Y as previously and more in terms of X. In the X sector, however, the same marginal physical productivity of labour as before will now earn less Y, due to the shift in relative prices. Hence labour in this sector

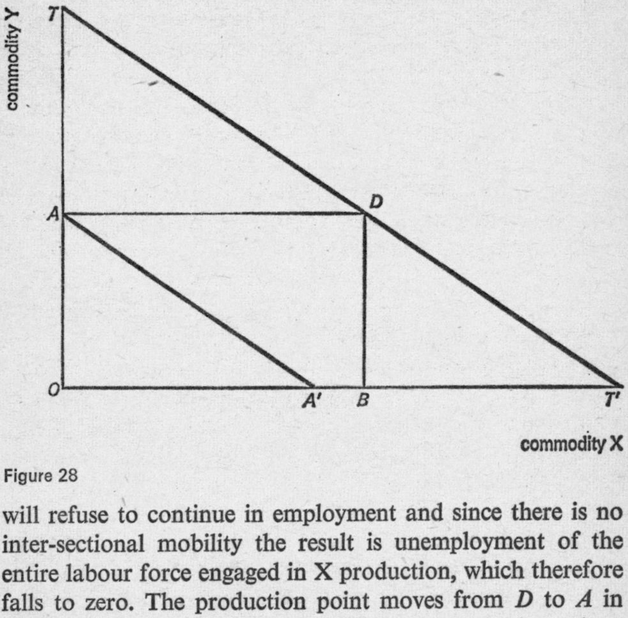

Figure 28

will refuse to continue in employment and since there is no inter-sectional mobility the result is unemployment of the entire labour force engaged in X production, which therefore falls to zero. The production point moves from *D* to *A* in Figure 28. Trade thus wipes out the X industry without there being any expansion in the Y industry.

Consumption-possibilities with trade will be determined by *OAA′* where the slope of *AA′*, parallel to *TT′*, is equal to the terms of trade. If the terms of trade are such that *A′* is to the left of *B* or coincides with it then the welfare frontier with trade will obviously lie entirely within the utility-possibility curve corresponding to autarky. No trade will be better than any trade in this case. If A' is to the right of B, however, there will be some points attainable with trade that are not under autarky so that the welfare frontiers will intersect, autarky being preferable for some income distributions and trade for others.

The factor immobility and price rigidity problem discussed here, and many other cases of the consequences of departure from the usual assumptions, was first examined by Haberler (1950). His analysis was refined and elaborated by Johnson (1965).

The formal theory of the gains from trade, with which we have been concerned in this chapter, is unfortunately restricted to a static context. Hence the vital contribution that the opportunity to specialize makes towards the dynamic transformation and development of an economy does not appear as one of the gains from trade, although this is undoubtedly of far greater significance than the mere pushing out of a utility-possibility curve. The gains from trade also go beyond the purely economic aspect of a nation's life since trading conditions and prospects greatly influence the social, political and cultural fabric of a nation as well. So far these aspects of the gains from trade have had to be left to the economic historians. It is to be hoped that the pure theory of the subject will advance sufficiently to take some account of these fundamental matters.

References

ARROW, K., CHENERY, H., MINHAS, B., and SOLOW, R. (1961), 'Capital-labour substitution and economic efficiency', *Review of Economics and Statistics*, vol. 43.

BALASSA, B. (1963), 'An empirical demonstration of classical comparative cost theory', *Review of Economics and Statistics*, vol. 45.

BALDWIN, R. E. (1948), 'Equilibrium in international trade: a diagrammatic analysis', *Quarterly Journal of Economics*, vol. 62.

BALDWIN, R. E. (1952), 'The new welfare economics and gains in international trade', *Quarterly Journal of Economics*, vol. 66.

BALL, D. S. (1966), 'Factor-intensity reversals in international comparison of factor costs and factor use', *Journal of Political Economy*, vol. 74.

BALOGH, T. (1963), *Unequal Partners*, Blackwell.

BECKER, G. S. (1952), 'A note on multi-country trade', *American Economic Review*, vol. 42.

BHAGWATI, J. (1964), 'The pure theory of international trade', *Economic Journal*, vol. 74.

BHARADWAJ, R. (1962), *Structural Basis of India's Foreign Trade*, Bombay.

CAVES, R. (1960), *Trade and Economic Structure*, Harvard University Press.

CHIPMAN, J. S. (1965, 1966), 'A survey of the theory of international trade', *Econometrica*, vols. 33 and 34.

ELLSWORTH, P. T. (1954), 'The structure of American foreign trade: a new view examined', *Review of Economics and Statistics*, vol. 36.

GRAAFF, J. DE V. (1957), *Theoretical Welfare Economics*, Cambridge University Press.

GRAHAM, F. D. (1948), *The Theory of International Values*, Princeton University Press.

GRUBER, W., MEHTA, D., and VERNON, R. (1967), 'The R & D factor in international trade and international investment of U.S. industries', *Journal of Political Economy*, vol. 75.

HABERLER, G. (1950), 'Some problems in the pure theory of international trade', *Economic Journal*, vol. 60.

HECKSCHER, E. (1949), 'The effect of foreign trade on the distribution of income', in H. S. Ellis and L. A. Metzler (eds.), *Readings in the Theory of International Trade*, Blakiston.

HOUTHAKKER, H. S. (1957), 'An international comparison of household expenditure patterns, commemorating the centenary of Engel's law', *Econometrica*, vol. 25.

JOHNSON, H. G. (1965), 'Optimal trade intervention in the presence of domestic distortions', in Baldwin *et al.*, *Trade, Growth and the Balance of Payments*, Rand McNally.

JONES, R. (1956), 'Factor endowment and the Heckscher-Ohlin model', *Review of Economic Studies*, vol. 24.

KEESING, D. (1967), 'The impact of research and development on United States trade', *Journal of Political Economy*, vol. 75.

KEMP, M. C. (1964), 'The gain from international trade', *Economic Journal*, vol. 74.

KENEN, P. B. (1965), 'Nature, capital and trade', *Journal of Political Economy*, vol. 73.

KINDLEBERGER, C. P. (1962), *Foreign Trade and the National Economy*, Yale University Press.

KRAVIS, I. B. (1956), 'Availability and other influences on the commodity composition of trade', *Journal of Political Economy*, vol. 64.

LEONTIEF, W. (1953), 'Domestic production and foreign trade: the American capital position re-examined', *Proceedings of the American Philosophical Society*.

LEONTIEF, W. (1956), 'Factor proportions and the structure of American trade: further theoretical and empirical analysis', *Review of Economics and Statistics*, vol. 38.

LEONTIEF, W. (1964), 'International factor cost and factor use', *American Economic Review*, vol. 54.

LERNER, A. P. (1952), 'Factor prices and international trade', *Economica*, vol. 19.

LEWIS, W. A. (1954), 'Economic development with unlimited supplies of labour', *Manchester School*, vol. 22.

LINDER, S. B. (1961), *An Essay on Trade and Transformation*, Wiley.

MACDOUGALL, G. D. A. (1951, 1952), 'British and American exports: a study suggested by the theory of comparative costs', *Economic Journal*, parts 1 and 2, vols. 61 and 62.

MINHAS, B. S. (1963), *An International Comparison of Factor Costs and Factor Use*, North Holland.

MISHAN, E. J. (1960), 'A survey of welfare economics 1939–59', *Economic Journal*, vol. 70.

MORONEY, J. R. (1967), 'The strong factor-intensity hypothesis: a multi-sectoral test', *Journal of Political Economy*, vol. 75.

MORONEY, J. R., and WALKER, J. M. (1966), 'A regional test of the Heckscher-Ohlin hypothesis', *Journal of Political Economy*, vol. 74.

MOSAK, J. L. (1944), *General Equilibrium Theory in International Trade*, Principia Press.

MYINT, H. (1958), 'The classical theory of international trade and the underdeveloped countries', *Economic Journal*, vol. 68.

NAYA, S. (1967), 'Natural resources, factor mix, and factor reversal in international trade', *American Economic Review*, vol. 57.

OHLIN, B. (1933), *Inter-regional and International Trade*, Harvard University Press.

POSNER, M. V. (1961), 'Technical change and international trade', *Oxford Economic Papers*, no. 13.

ROBINSON, R. (1956), 'Factor proportions and comparative advantage: part 1', *Quarterly Journal of Economics*, vol. 70.

RYBCZYNSKI, T. M. (1955), 'Factor endowment and relative commodity prices', *Economica*, vol. 22.

SAMUELSON, P. A. (1939), 'The gains from international trade', *Canadian Journal of Economics and Political Science*, vol. 5.

SAMUELSON, P. A. (1950), 'The evaluation of real national income', *Oxford Economic Papers*, no. 2.

SAMUELSON, P. A. (1951–2), 'A comment on factor price equalization', *Review of Economic Studies*, vol. 19(2), no. 49.

SAMUELSON, P. A. (1964), 'The gains from international trade once again', *Economic Journal*, vol. 74.

SCITOVSKY, T. (1942), 'A reconsideration of the theory of tariffs', *Review of Economic Studies*, vol. 10.

STERN, R. (1962), 'British and American productivity and comparative costs in international trade', *Oxford Economic Papers*, no. 14.

STOLPER, W. F., and SAMUELSON, P. A. (1941), 'Protection and real wages', *Review of Economic Studies*, vol. 9.

SWERLING, B. C. (1954), 'Capital shortage and labour surplus in the United States', *Review of Economics and Statistics*, vol. 36.

VALVANIS-VAIL, S. (1954), 'Leontief's scarce factor paradox', *Journal of Political Economy*, vol. 62.

VANEK, J. (1963), *The Natural Resource Content of United States Foreign Trade 1870–1955*, M.I.T. Press.

VINER, J. (1937), *Studies in the Theory of International Trade*, Harper.

WAHL, D. F. (1961), 'Capital and labour requirements for Canada's foreign trade', *Canadian Journal of Economics and Political Science*, vol. 27.

WILLIAMS, J. H. (1929), 'The theory of international trade reconsidered', *Economic Journal*, vol. 39.

Index

Penguin Modern Economics Texts

A new series of short, original unit texts on various aspects of thought and research in important areas of economics. The series is under the general editorship of B. J. McCormick, Senior Lecturer in Economics, University of Sheffield

Balance-of-Payments Policy
B. J. Cohen

The Control of the Money Supply
A. D. Bain

The Economics of Agriculture
David Metcalf

The Economics of the Common Market
D. Swann

Elements of Regional Economics
Harry W. Richardson

Industrial Concentration
M. A. Utton

The International Monetary System
Herbert G. Grubel

Nationalized Industries
Graham L. Reid and Kevin Allen

The Principles of Development Aid
E. K. Hawkins

The Theory of Taxation
Charles M. Allan

Wages
B. J. McCormick

Penguin Modern Economics Readings

Economics of Education
Volumes 1 and 2
Edited by M. Blaug

Economic Policy for Development
Edited by I. Livingstone

Economics of Technicological Change
Edited by Nathan Rosenberg

Foreign Aid
Edited by Jagdish Bhagwati and Richard S. Eckaus

Growth Economics
Edited by Amartya Sen

Inflation
Edited by R. J. Ball and Peter Doyle

International Finance
Edited by R. N. Cooper

International Trade
Edited by Jagdish Bhagwati

The Labour Market
Edited by B. J. McCormick and E. Owen Smith

Managerial Economics
Edited by G. P. E. Clarkson

Monetary Theory
Edited by R. W. Clower

Monopoly and Competition
Edited by Alex Hunter

Power in Economics
Edited by K. W. Rothschild

Public Enterprise
Edited by R. Turvey

Public Finance
Edited by R. W. Houghton

Regional Analysis
Edited by L. Needleman

Transport
Edited by Denys Munby